Patrick Regan OBE is an activist, author and speaker who writes about resilience, courage and wellbeing. He has founded two award-winning charities – XLP and, most recently, Kintsugi Hope in partnership with his wife, Diane. Kintsugi Hope has pioneered Kintsugi Wellbeing Groups all over the UK to help people in the area of their mental health. Patrick is a mental health first aider and a campaigner on issues of social justice, and was awarded an OBE for his services to the young by Her Late Majesty Queen Elizabeth II. He is an Honorary Fellow of the South Bank University for his contribution to Justice and Wellbeing. Patrick has written seven books. His other titles cover his work with tackling poverty and educational failure, and his own journey with mental, emotional and spiritual health following major limb reconstruction surgery. Patrick is also a director of Brighter Days (https://www.brighterdays.life), providing high-quality training on well-being in the workplace, educational settings and local authorities. Patrick is married to Diane, and they have four children. Find out more on Twitter: @patrickregankh and Instagram: @patrickregan2726.

Liza Hoeksma is a writer who has worked with a number of authors. She has partnered with Patrick Regan on all seven of his books to date. She works in communications for a charity based in Hertfordshire as well as being a life coach, working with clients across the country. Find out more at www.coachingwithliza.com and on Instagram: @Coaching_with_Liza.

When Faith Gets Shaken

'A moving story of courage and faith'
Bear Grylls

Patrick Regan
with Liza Hoeksma

spck

First published in the UK in 2015
by CWR

This edition published in Great Britain in 2024

SPCK
SPCK Group
Studio 101
The Record Hall
16–16A Baldwin's Gardens
London EC1N 7RJ

www.spck.org.uk

Copyright © Patrick Regan and Liza Hoeksma 2024

Patrick Regan and Liza Hoeksma have asserted their right under the Copyright, Designs and Patents Act, 1988, to be identified as Authors of this work.

All rights reserved. No part of this book may be reproduced or transmitted in any form or by any means, electronic or mechanical, including photocopying, recording, or by any information storage and retrieval system, without permission in writing from the publisher.

SPCK does not necessarily endorse the individual views contained in its publications.

The author and publisher have made every effort to ensure that the external website and email addresses included in this book are correct and up to date at the time of going to press. The author and publisher are not responsible for the content, quality or continuing accessibility of the sites.

Unless otherwise noted, Scripture quotations are taken from the HOLY BIBLE, NEW INTERNATIONAL VERSION. Copyright © 1973, 1978, 1984 by International Bible Society. Used by permission of Hodder & Stoughton Publishers, a member of the Hachette UK Group. All rights reserved. 'NIV' is a registered trademark of International Bible Society. UK trademark number 1448790.

Scripture quotations marked "*The Message*" are taken from The Message, copyright © 1993, 1994, 1995, 1996, 2000, 2001, 2002. Used by permission of NavPress Publishing Group.

Scripture quotations from The Authorized (King James) Version: rights in the Authorized Version in the United Kingdom are vested in the Crown. Reproduced by permission of the Crown's patentee, Cambridge University Press.

p. 89 Extract from "From the Inside Out", words and music by Joel Houston copyright © 2005 Hillsong Music Publishing. Reprinted by permission of Hillsong Music Publishing.

British Library Cataloguing-in-Publication Data
A catalogue record for this book is available from the British Library

ISBN 978–0–281–08990–1
eBook ISBN 978–0–281–08991–8
audio download 978–0–281–08992–5

1 3 5 7 9 10 8 6 4 2

Typeset by Fakenham Prepress Solutions, Fakenham, Norfolk, NR21 8NL
First printed in Great Britain by Clays Ltd, Bungay, Suffolk, NR35 1ED
Subsequently digitally printed in Great Britain
eBook by Fakenham Prepress Solutions, Fakenham, Norfolk, NR21 8NL
Produced on paper from sustainable forests

*To Diane, Keziah, Daniel, Abigail, and Caleb:
I'm so proud to be your husband and dad; in sickness and in
health you have all been my rock.*

CONTENTS

Introduction: Will I Hold on to My Faith?	9
1 God, Where are You?	15
2 Peace	31
Andy's Story	**44**
3 Rethinking Courage	52
4 Standing Stubbornly Nowhere	62
Liza's Story	**74**
5 Broken Yet Held Together by Love	82
6 Running on Empty	93
7 Second-hand Smoke: Diane's Story	104
8 Guilt	112
Hannah's Story	**123**
9 Anger	135
10 Dreaming Again	146
11 VSP	160
Epilogue: Beauty from Brokenness	168

INTRODUCTION

Will I Hold on to My Faith?

Have you ever struggled with your faith? I mean *really* struggled? Not just an occasional fleeting doubt but a season of your life when you wrestled with the very nature and existence of God: is he good? Is he kind? Does he care? Is he in control? Is he even there? Facing suffering, and seeing others suffer, can break our hearts and pierce the very core of our faith, but it doesn't have to be the final word in our lives.

Moody Bible College President Joseph Stowell tells the story of the night he met Billy Graham,[1] the renowned evangelist who has seen thousands upon thousands come to faith. They had been at a dinner together and, after the meal, Stowell managed to ask the question he'd been longing to ask all evening: "Of all of your experiences in ministry," he said, "what have you enjoyed the most?" He wondered aloud if it would be time spent with presidents and heads of state, but Graham quickly pushed his suggestion aside and said, "By far the greatest joy of my life has been fellowship with Jesus. Hearing Him speak to me, having Him guide me, sensing His

---

[1] Joseph M. Stowell, *Simply Jesus*, Colorado Springs, CO: Multnomah Publishers, Inc., 2002, page 16.

presence with me and His power through me. This has been the highest pleasure of my life!" The response was unscripted, unrehearsed, and clearly from the heart. Graham didn't even have to pause to look back over the then eighty years of his life to draw that conclusion; his relationship with Jesus beat everything else hands down.

In contrast, author Lee Strobel tells of meeting one of Billy Graham's friends, Chuck Templeton, who was himself a well-known evangelist and who ministered alongside Graham in setting up Youth for Christ Canada. Having brought many to faith, Templeton eventually denounced that faith and wrote *Farewell to God*, a book outlining why he had shunned his previous beliefs. Strobel said that Templeton, who was then eighty-three and in declining health, just couldn't reconcile a God who said he was love with the horrendous amount of suffering he permitted in the world. He stood by his decision to turn his back on the Christian faith. But when Strobel asked how he felt about Jesus, Templeton, he said, visibly softened and spoke of Jesus in adoring terms. He said, "In my view he is the most important human being who has ever existed." His voice cracked, and he added haltingly, "I... miss... him," before he began to weep.

Billy Graham and Chuck Templeton were two friends who worked together to introduce people to Jesus. But as they grew older their lives couldn't have been more different, Graham rating his relationship with Jesus far above anything else he had witnessed or experienced on earth, Templeton weeping for the man he had loved and lost.

This story has always struck fear into my heart. What if I end up like Templeton, so overwhelmed by the pain and suffering in the world that I can no longer believe in a loving and powerful God? It's not the sort of thing Christian leaders are supposed to say, is it? Certainly not publicly. But I see so much agony around me that sometimes, like Templeton, I find it hard to reconcile this with who I understand God to be. I've worked with young people for around twenty-two years and I've seen so much heartbreak. I regularly speak to mothers whose children have been stabbed and left to bleed to death on the streets. I deal with kids who have been emotionally, physically, and sexually abused by the adults who are supposed to take care of them. I've held children who weeks later have died from a preventable disease because they live in countries where there is such poverty that they don't have access to the simple medicines that would have saved their lives. These things take their toll and there's no way to protect yourself from the horror of so much pain and suffering. I know a powerful God and yet I feel helpless. I'm desperate to make things better, and I believe that is God's heart, but how can you bring back the dead to life, rewind time and protect children, or provide food and medicine for every child living in poverty?

Many of us know the theological answers to some of the big questions about why people suffer. I know I've read about them, wrestled with them, prayed about them, and even preached on them, but nothing makes it any easier when you're staring suffering in the face. That's why this book isn't about the "whys" of suffering. There are far more theologically minded people than me who can help you if that's your question. This book is about how we deal with suffering when it comes and rocks our world. It's an honest look at what we do when everything falls apart and we're left with very few certainties. It's about how we keep going when we're faced with physical, emotional, and psychological pain in our own lives and in the lives of those we love. It's about learning that God is with us even when it doesn't feel like it. It's about how we stay present in the moment rather than wishing our lives away, waiting for a day when things will be better. It's about being kind to ourselves and allowing ourselves the grace to rest; and encouraging us to be vulnerable with one another so that those around us can see who we truly are. It's about how we find peace when life is anything but peaceful, and ultimately about how we grasp the love of God at a deeper level.

If you have read any of my other books or heard me speak, you'll know that I often talk about things like how I've worked with gangs in Jamaica's Trench Town and on the streets of Los Angeles. I've spent time in some of the world's poorest places, such as India, Bolivia, Ghana, and Asia, and seen Christians doing amazing things while working with communities to relieve poverty and bring transformation. I can share stories of change from my hometown of London, where urban youth charity XLP works each week with almost 2,000 young people who are at risk of exclusion from school and of getting into gangs. I've met some of the country's most high-profile political leaders and been consulted on a number of issues to speak up for the young people we work with.

As preachers we're good at telling these stories, and they are often what people want to hear; I know that when I listen to a speaker, I want to be encouraged and inspired by the things that God does in our world. Those stories are important to tell and we need to hear from as many people as we can about ways in which we see God at work. But sometimes we can hear other people's amazing stories and wonder why our life doesn't match up, forgetting that this is never the full

Will I Hold on to My Faith?

picture. Pastor Steven Furtick says, "The reason we struggle with insecurity is that we compare our behind-the-scenes with everyone else's highlight reel." Isn't that true? We look at preachers and think their life is great because they have these amazing stories to tell, forgetting that they are just giving us their highlights because they want to inspire us. Their everyday lives probably aren't all that different from ours. They still get sick, have bad days at work, wonder why their prayers haven't been answered, argue with their spouse, clean up after their kids, have to navigate complex friendships, and wrestle with doubts and insecurities. They have to do many of the same mundane daily activities that we do, and struggle with problems and setbacks, but, from the twenty minutes of their lives that we hear about from their talks, we think they simply go from one glorious God-encounter to another.

I know I feel challenged to make sure my talks are now more balanced so that people also hear stories that highlight our common humanity, and that's partly why I wrote this book. I want to tell you a bit about what's been going on in my life behind the scenes while some of the other stuff that I've written about was going on. Not because I think my life is all that interesting or to use this as a form of cheap therapy, but because God has taken me on a journey that I think many of you are on too. While I've seen God doing amazing things in London and all around the world, my faith has been shaken to the core by the pain and suffering in my own life and in the lives of those I love. As I have shared my struggles and some of God's whispers with people I've met who are suffering and struggling, they have seemed to strike a chord, so my hope and prayer is that they will do the same for you. There is something very powerful in us being honest about where we're at and the things we find difficult. I've read many books where people have talked about how amazing it is to come out the other side of suffering and see with hindsight all the wonderful things that God was doing, but I wanted to write while I was still in the process of dealing with the pain. Because the truth is I'm still grappling with these issues. I'm still trying to figure out where God is and what he's doing. He's been whispering to me along the way but I'm not always that good at stopping and listening. I foolishly try to sort things out using my own resources and then get increasingly frustrated when I realize that I don't have the required strength to do it all on my own.

Life is complex and we are more fragile than we sometimes realize. When I'm in pain, and I see those around me suffering, I sometimes lose sight of God. But when I strip everything back – my past experiences, my frustrations, my fears of being misunderstood – I realize that I need to look again at the person of Jesus. When I see him, I find hope. I remember that he really is willing to get involved in the agonies of our lives and to go through the pain with us. He doesn't leave us on our own to figure things out and he's desperate for us to know how much he loves us. When I remember that I find myself wanting not to abandon ship but to be part of the journey. In the process of that journey, I am slowly learning to let Jesus speak to me about his love for me and for the world. I need to stay as close to him as I can, walking beside him even if I'm walking with the limp of confusion and doubt, because I love him. Templeton's story serves as a warning to us that this is where we need to be and this is where we need to stay. We have to keep looking to Jesus so that we never walk away from our faith and find ourselves in the heartbreaking position of having to say, "I miss him."

Chapter 1

God, Where are You?

I've always considered myself to be someone with a solid faith. I grew up knowing that both my parents and my sister loved Jesus and were committed to living every area of their lives for him. I was no stranger to stories of God healing people dramatically, and in fact God healed me of jaundice and complications related to Rh incompatibility when I was born. My mum also tells me that when I was four she found my baby sister cold and unresponsive in her cot. While she ran to phone for an ambulance, I apparently knelt down to pray, and by the time she came back upstairs my sister was smiling and giggling as though nothing had ever been wrong. But my family also knew, all too well, that God doesn't always answer prayers for healing with a yes. When I was very young, my brother Matthew died when he was just a few days old. It was the day before my birthday, so every year as I celebrated getting a year older I thought about what it would have been like if he'd lived and we'd been able to grow up together. Matthew's death was incredibly painful for my whole family but my parents managed to hold tight to their faith and set me an incredible example to follow.

As I got older, I knew that I wanted to live for Jesus

When Faith Gets Shaken

and do whatever he called me to. I was passionate about communicating and telling others about God through both my words and my actions, dragging teenage friends along to Christian gigs, putting on video shows and non-alcoholic cocktail evenings – anything that would help me introduce others to my faith. I met Diane, my wife, at school when I was just fifteen. She also loved Jesus and we got married when I was twenty-one. When I finished studying, I did a missional gap year and began doing youth work for a local church in London. When I was invited to speak at a local school after a pupil was stabbed, it led me to set up a charity, XLP. Though life had its ups and downs and starting a charity presented a whole set of challenges I had never expected, life was pretty good. I began to travel to understand the cultures of the kids I was working with, I was asked to speak at different churches and events all over the place, and Diane and I started a family.

When our first child, Keziah, was born, there were complications and she was in special care for ten days. It was so hard to see our tiny and precious daughter so seriously ill, but thankfully she recovered well. A few years later when Diane was pregnant with our second child, Daniel, we found out at twenty-three weeks that he had a two-cord artery instead of three, and this was potentially indicative of a major chromosomal problem. Again we feared for our child, but he was born healthy and our fears were allayed. Situations like these give you wobbles in your faith but in isolation you can deal with them; I just wasn't prepared for what was ahead.

About six years ago things started to go seriously wrong. Keziah was just five when she started complaining of severe pain in her stomach and her joints and then came out in a rash on her legs that looked like purple/brown bruises. It turned out to be a rare condition called Henoch-Schönlein purpura (HSP), which affects children and means their immune system isn't working properly. The doctor was fascinated, calling in a colleague to take a look as neither had seen the condition before. It can cause the kidneys to stop working properly so we had to monitor Keziah's urine and twice we found traces of protein. I'll confess that my first reaction in this type of situation is to panic. I hate being out of control and there are few things as frightening as seeing your child in pain and not being able to make them better. The doctor came to our home to check on Keziah and I was desperate for her to come up with some sort of miracle cure. I wanted instant results but, when it comes to healing, it can be a slow process. In fear I said to the doctor, "It's not life-threatening, is it?", waiting for her to tell me I was overreacting. Instead, she said, "It can be. You need to take her to hospital." To our relief the hospital discharged her, but it wasn't long before we were rushing her back in after she developed a fever and was sick. There's never a good time to be ill, but that visit happened to be on Boxing Day and the joy was certainly sucked out of our family celebrations as we waited to see if Keziah would be OK. Over a period of six weeks we were in and out of A&E every weekend, and it wasn't just with Keziah. We decided to take a break at Center Parcs to have some time together as a family, but when our son Daniel was coming down the flume another kid crashed into him. Daniel broke his leg, so it was back to A&E for us and back to crawling for a few weeks for Daniel.

A few months later our third child, Abigail, was born and all was well. "At last," we thought, "a pregnancy and birth with no complications!" When she was ten weeks old, both Keziah and Daniel were on antibiotics for an ear infection and late on a Friday night we suspected that Abigail was infected too. To save waiting until the Monday for a doctor's appointment, Diane took Abigail to A&E to have her checked that evening. While there she was alarmed when the doctor who was assessing Abigail thought she was blind. She was waving a pen in front of Abigail's eyes and commenting on her lack of interest. Diane picked up a brightly coloured toy and dangled it close to Abigail for her to respond to, which she did. The doctor asked if we had noticed Abigail's eyes flickering. We had, but had just thought she was taking everything in very quickly. The doctor said she probably had an eye condition called nystagmus, which is a problem in the pathways between the brain and the eyes that causes difficulties with vision that can't be corrected by glasses. She warned that it could also be a sign of something quite serious. We were distraught. We looked up information online and found websites saying that this diagnosis wasn't the end of the world (despite it feeling that way). Tests confirmed she had nystagmus (anything more sinister was thankfully ruled out), but they said there was little they could do except monitor her to see what happened. She can currently see about six metres ahead of her (a normally sighted child can see double that), and can see clearly only by looking out at an angle. We don't know how this will affect her in the future and she continues to have hospital tests every few months and a visual aid expert to visit her termly in school to monitor the situation.

It wasn't just the kids who were in and out of hospital either. I was struggling with pain in my knees, and as I'd been a keen footballer for many years, I wondered if it was an old injury flaring up. After an MRI scan I discovered that the truth was far worse: I had a degenerative knee condition that would require major limb reconstruction surgery. I listened in horror as the consultant described how they would have to break my legs above the ankle and below the knee. Then they would attach a huge circular metal frame with three metal rings circling my leg at the ankle, shin, and just below the knee. These rings would be linked by twelve metal struts that would have to be moved slowly to set the bones correctly and to allow the bone to grow into the gaps created. To keep everything in place there would be six large pins going right through my bones, and another six that would be screwed into the bones. The frame would be on for a minimum of six months, and once it came off I still wouldn't be able to walk for a while. The even worse news was that, as both my knees were affected, they would have to repeat the operation for the second leg once I had recovered from the first operation. The whole process meant two or three years of pain and major disruption to my life.

I was devastated. I asked if there were any other options and was assured this was it. If I had been older they would have given me a straightforward knee replacement, which is much less invasive and has a much shorter recovery time. The downside to knee replacement surgery is that the effects don't last for ever and it can be done only once or twice, so they won't do it for anyone under fifty. As I was diagnosed in my thirties, they said I would have to have the limb reconstruction now, and when that was no longer sufficient, I would have to have the knee replacement surgery too.

I found it hard to take in the implications of what I was being told. I had no idea what my life was going to look like if I couldn't walk. I started XLP in 1996 and we now run projects in schools and communities across seven London boroughs, reaching almost 2,000 young people every week. There is so much need and always so much going on. The team are amazing but things are always busy and there's never a good time to take a break. Life at home was busy too with three young kids. How would I be able to look after them or play with them if I wasn't mobile? Football had always been a big part of my life and a much-needed stress outlet and now I was being told I couldn't play any more. I would be in pain and have limited mobility for a long time.

When they showed me what the frame was like, the horror grew. The pins and screws that held it in place looked as if they'd cause agony, and the frame was so huge there would no hiding it. I could remember seeing people with them on in the past and had thought to myself then that it would be my worst nightmare. I'm quite a self-conscious person so the last thing I wanted was to have such an obvious sign that no one could miss, advertising the fact there was something wrong with my leg. I asked the doctors when I would need the operation and their response didn't cheer me up. They said that they would wait until I was in agony before they would perform it. Their experience is that the pain after the operation can be endured only if the patient knows they are ultimately being saved from excruciating pain in their everyday life.

It was a very strange thing knowing there was a major operation looming on the horizon but that I couldn't even plan for when it would be. All I knew was that that my pain was going to increase until I eventually walked into a hospital to have my legs voluntarily broken. Then I would have to endure months of a painful recovery process before doing it all again. As one of my friends commented, it was like waiting for a horrendous car crash you knew for certain was going to happen.

I found the uncertainty of the timing very difficult. I'm a visionary and I love to make plans for the future; suddenly my future seemed to offer nothing but a series of operations. Diane and I had been talking about having another child and suddenly we didn't know how that would work with my operations. After much discussion we decided to try for another baby straight away and hope that my knees would hold out for a bit longer. The one bright spot on the horizon appeared when we found out Diane was pregnant. We were overjoyed, and at last there seemed to be some good news.

But then my dad got some terrible news: he had bowel cancer. We've always been a close family and we were all rocked by the thought of Dad's life being threatened. An operation was planned to remove the tumour and we were told he should be home within a week. After the procedure we were given good and bad news. Thankfully, the cancer hadn't spread, so his long-term prognosis was good; that was a huge relief for all of us. But unfortunately during the operation they had cut through Dad's urethra by mistake, leaving him in a lot of pain. Things worsened when they said his bowel was twisted and he had a blood clot; he needed a stent but the only person who could do it was away for two weeks. Dad was in hospital in Essex, and for me to travel from London took about an hour and a half each way. Every time I made the journey I would pray that he'd be sitting up and looking healthier, but every day when I got to his bedside he looked a little worse. He lost three stone and, as he wasn't a heavy man to begin with, he looked gaunt and fragile. My prayers consisted largely of my begging God not to let him die. My dad has a strong faith and one of his favourite sayings is "You can't have a victory without a battle". He didn't waver in his understanding of God's goodness or his love. I wish I could say the same as I watched him spend nine weeks in hospital, in terrible pain, getting weaker and weaker when he should have been almost fully recovered.

More bad news was to come. While I was going backwards and forwards to the hospital, Diane suffered a miscarriage. She had been thirteen weeks along in the pregnancy and we were devastated. It's a very hard thing to process, losing a child that you haven't even met. Diane couldn't talk about it without crying and I didn't know how to get my head around it. We knew that miscarriage is common but of course that doesn't mean it's any less painful when it happens. We grieved for the child we would never know and both feared that we'd missed our last chance to have another baby before I went into hospital for my leg operation.

I desperately wanted to be as steadfast and faith-filled as my dad but I'll be honest – I got very low. The question I kept asking God is probably familiar to many people who've faced difficult situations: "Why me?" I wanted to list all the good things I'd done in my life, all the ways I'd tried to serve God and bless my community, and come up with all the reasons why none of this should be happening to me or my family. Rationally I knew that life doesn't work like that, but it's very hard to be rational when there are so many painful things happening and you can't see where God is in the midst of them.

It wasn't just me either. I found that other Christians were struggling to know how to respond too. One person sent a text to my dad while he lay in hospital, saying, "I'm speaking to the cancer and it is now gone in Jesus' name." I'm sure they had the best intentions, but it wasn't exactly helpful. Many friends were praying for my knees to be healed too. Whenever I was speaking somewhere, the team there would ask to pray for me, or would invite a guest speaker known to have a healing ministry to try. I was invited to healing meetings and prayed for at every opportunity. After they'd prayed, I would often be asked, "How does it feel? Can you do something now that you couldn't do before?" As I looked at their expectant faces, I wished I could say all the pain was gone and that I was fully healed. It became embarrassing to say time and time again that nothing had changed, and I would apologize profusely as though I had let them down. No matter how often I was prayed for my leg was still bowed, and, though the pain came and went, it was showing no signs of improvement. Some people told me that it was my fault I wasn't healed because I didn't have enough faith, and others claimed that "speakers are the worst people for receiving". Trying to encourage me, people commented, "God will use the time you have after your operation to teach you how to rest," or said, "Think of all the time you'll have on your hands to pray and be in God's presence!" Many people told me about times of trial they had been through (ranging from bad flu to a broken ankle) and told me they had known God more closely in their suffering. While I was glad for them that they were able to testify to God's presence in their pain, our stories were different and I didn't find it all that reassuring. Someone even told me, "God has backed you into a corner to teach you something." That conjured up some pretty unhelpful images of God in my mind! During charismatic meetings it seemed as if there was always a story about someone being miraculously healed, whether that was someone getting out of wheelchair or a dead person being raised to life. I didn't begrudge anyone their healing – I loved knowing God was doing miraculous things – but you do find yourself asking, "What's wrong with *me*? Why aren't *I* being healed?"

If you've read one of my previous books, you'll know I'm a firm believer in having hope against all odds. At XLP we work with young people who have chaotic lifestyles and whom others have written off. We regularly say that hope is the refusal to accept a situation as it is. I've visited some of the world's poorest areas and seen God's light shining in even the darkest places. I believe with all my heart that God wants to restore this world, and when it comes to other people's circumstances, I can dream of a better future. It's when it comes to my own life that I can often struggle to find that same perspective. My last book was all about hope, and as I spoke on that theme in front of hundreds of people, and even to millions of people through national TV and newspapers, I would wonder whether I was a complete hypocrite when I felt so hopeless about my own life.

My anxiety was growing, and that was making me feel guilty. I knew I should be able to bring my troubles to God and felt that I was letting people down by being a Christian leader who was struggling with so many doubts and worries. My family could see I was spiralling downwards and tried their best to support me, but the anxiety started taking a toll on my health. I began getting new aches and pains, and when I searched online to do a bit of self-diagnosis the conclusion was always that I had some sort of terminal disease. Google was really not my friend! I considered taking antidepressants, to help me through a difficult time. I know some Christians have a problem with them, but I don't believe depression, anxiety, and panic attacks are a sign of weakness or that there should be any stigma attached to taking medication for them. Statistics show that one in three of us will suffer in these areas at some point in our life. Eventually I decided the best route for me was to see a professional counsellor to chat to them about the best way forward, whether that was medication or anything else. Part of me was sceptical about whether talking to a stranger would help, but a Christian friend who is a psychiatrist persuaded me to give it a try.

I was a little nervous about how my first counselling session would go, but quickly realized it was going to be extremely helpful. By nature I'm a solutions man, so when I'm presented with a problem my instinct is to try to jump in with ten ideas on how to solve the problem. What I wasn't giving myself time for was to have my current feelings validated before I was in a position to think about possible solutions. That's one of the amazing things about counsellors: they listen and let you talk without judging you and trying to move you on before you're ready. I thought I needed an action plan for how to get through a painful season in my life but what I needed before that was someone to tell me it was OK that I was finding things hard and that I hadn't already "prayed myself through to victory". I needed to let go of the guilt that had crept in about whether I hadn't been healed because of a lack of faith. My counsellor helped me to realize that I needed to be kinder to myself. I continually set myself incredibly high standards that I can't possibly hope to meet, and then beat myself up for not reaching them. As a Christian, my counsellor had lots of experience with Christian leaders who had pushed themselves beyond reasonable limits in the name of advancing God's mission. She would often ask, "Do you feel God in any of this?" and I felt that I was supposed to say yes, but my honest answer was, "I don't know." In my naïvety I thought I'd be sorted with five or six sessions; I was looking for an instant fix, but it didn't work out that way.

As I started to let go of the pressures I was piling on myself, I began to see that God really was with me in the turmoil. Because of all the stress I hadn't been sleeping very well, and if you tell that to someone who knows their Bible they will often quote Psalm 127:2, which says that God "grants sleep to those he loves". When you're feeling anxious and sleep-deprived, the last thing you need is to think that you're not even loved by God! One morning, after another night of tossing and turning, I came across Psalm 56:8 in *The Message*, which says, "You've kept track of my every toss and turn through the sleepless nights." What a relief! God wasn't waiting for me to get over my crisis of faith, angry with me that I couldn't summon the trust to see his good plans in among all the awful stuff that was happening. He was with me during my sleepless nights of anxiety and pain as I tried to figure everything out.

God, Where are You?

It's so easy to lose sight of who God is when things are hard. A quote from *The Shack* always sticks in my mind: *The Shack* is a fictional tale by William Paul Young of a man meeting God in the pain of losing his child, in which God says, "Just because I work incredible good out of unspeakable tragedies doesn't mean I orchestrate the tragedies. Don't ever assume that my using something means I caused it or that I need it to accomplish my purposes. That will only lead you to false notions about me."[2]

When our circumstances are painful and confusing, we focus a lot of our energy on asking why. We want answers; we want to know why things are happening to us and how they're going to turn out. But very few of us get the answers we want – we just get tangled up in knots. I take comfort from the stories of Mother Teresa, who was well known for her phenomenal acts of love and faith. When she was asked by a young man if she would pray for him to have clarity, she refused. She told him, "Clarity is the last thing you are clinging to and must let go of. I have never had clarity; what I have always had is trust. So I will pray you will trust God." As my knees deteriorated, that was the story I was holding on to. I couldn't understand why I was going to have to undergo such intensive surgery and prolonged recovery; I didn't know why God hadn't healed me despite all the prayers I and others had offered, but I could still choose whether or not to trust him. That much was under my control.

Instead of focusing on the whys and what-ifs, I knew I needed to remember who God is. He is Immanuel – God

---

[2] William P. Young, *The Shack*, Newbury Park, CA: Windblown Media, 2007, page 185.

with us. Psalm 23 (KJV) says "Though I walk through the valley of the shadow of death"; we would all prefer God to take us *around* the valley of the shadow of death, but instead we walk right through it. But the psalmist goes on to say that even in that dark place we don't need to fear evil. Not because evil isn't real, or because we should pretend that pain is OK, but because *God is with us*.

He is also the God who promises to use any situation for good (Romans 8:28). Some of you will have heard of Nick Vujicic, who was born without arms and legs. Though as a child he felt so hopeless that he attempted suicide, he has gone on to become a hugely inspirational example to millions around the world as he has shared a message of hope in Jesus. Because of the challenges he faces he has received thousands of emails from others, sharing their stories, and he says that many ask "Why me?" about the things they're going through. One letter he received really made an impact on me.[3] A guy called Jason was in a car with his family when the driver lost control and the car hit the crash barrier, flipping the vehicle over. Jason was thrown from the car and his skull was cracked as he hit the ground, damaging his brain in four places. Thankfully, a nearby ambulance was able to get to the scene quickly, but Jason still lay in a coma for two weeks. When he finally awoke, his right side was paralysed. He underwent rigorous rehabilitation for a month and managed to regain the ability to speak, but he still remained paralysed. Amazingly, when he wrote to Nick Vujicic, his question wasn't "Why me?", like so many others. He must have gone through the most incredible

---

[3] Nick Vujicic, *Unstoppable: The Incredible Power of Faith in Action*, Colorado Springs, CO: WaterBrook Press, 2012, page 107.

anguish as his whole life changed, and he said he feared no one would ever treat him the same way again. But he said he realized something that changed everything: God was with him and he would be OK. Jason said, "I used to ask 'Why me?'; now I ask, 'Why not me?'" When people asked him if he still believed in God, he replied, "God kept me alive; how could I not believe in him?" Nick commented, "I don't believe God causes us to be hurt, sick or to suffer a loss, but I do believe that God finds a way for us to use bad things for a good purpose." I agree. When we get stuck in the "why" questions, we're looking for answers that are unlikely to come; sometimes we have to let go and trust that God is working even in the awful circumstances of our lives, even when we can't see it.

Our faith can get shaken for many reasons. Often it's not just one terrible incident, but a culmination of many painful factors, whether that's a relationship breakdown, being damaged by church, the death of someone we love, an illness, a tragic event like 9/11, an earthquake or a tsunami, or an area of theology we can't get our head around. There can be an unspoken rule in the church that we don't talk about our doubts; we should just focus on our faith, but even a quick look at the Psalms will tell you that God has no problem with allowing people to express themselves honestly.

As a family we could still see God's goodness in many ways, not least in that Diane became pregnant again. So finally we were back in hospital for a joyful reason: to welcome our son Caleb into the world. We were so thankful for this gift of a fourth child that we had doubted we might ever get to love. The complication was that Diane ended up having an emergency Caesarean and lost almost three litres of blood. As she lay in bed in the high-dependency unit, her face yellow from the blood loss, our new son – just hours old – asleep in a cot next to her, I wondered why even this happy moment couldn't be straightforward. The hospital overlooked the headquarters of the Salvation Army and when I looked out of the window, I saw a huge cross lighting up the night sky. The truth hit me again that God allowed his only Son to die the most painful and horrendous death for us. Why would he show us his love through the ultimate act of sacrifice, only to leave us in our times of need? I remembered again that God was with me whether I could feel his presence or not. The years of turmoil had shown me that we can't always plan life and there are many, many things that are outside our control, but we can be sure that, whether we feel it or not, God hasn't left us. So, after five years of going backwards and forwards, praying about when to have surgery, I finally decided it was time to put myself on the waiting list and have the operation.

Chapter 2

Peace

The summer before my operation was manic. I got it into my head that as I was going to be out of action for a long time, I should cram in as much as possible before I went into hospital. I kept pushing myself, ignoring the fact that this was clearly a terrible strategy. I was already feeling low, and getting exhausted wasn't going to help, but it was an exciting time for XLP as we were launching a national mentoring programme. I was desperate to get the message out as widely as we could so that the church could help as many young people as possible. I spoke at churches and events, saying yes to every invitation because I knew I was going to have to say no for a long time. Every time I went somewhere new I would get asked about my knees, and time and time again I ran through the problems I had and the procedures that awaited me, both feeling tired of retelling the same story and wincing internally every time I mentioned the pins that would go right through my bones. Everyone had different opinions about what I should do and many wondered aloud why God hadn't healed me, making me confront that painful question sometimes multiple times a day.

One night at a festival I just couldn't take any more.

There had been some amazing healings going on among the delegates, and although I was truly happy for those people, it only served to remind me that God wasn't healing *me*. The only conclusion my exhausted brain could jump to was that I wasn't important enough for God to heal me. So, while thousands celebrated and praised Jesus, I sneaked back to my B&B so I wouldn't have to face anyone. As I sat there I began to question my trust in God. Every time I received prayer for my knee, people would first ask for miraculous healing, and then, when that didn't happen, they would pray that I could trust God. I wondered how strong my faith really was. Could it cope with the physical, emotional, and professional challenges that were being thrown my way? We sing about trusting God and we memorize verses from the Bible about trust, but when it comes down to it, do I actually trust an invisible God with every area of my life? It's easy to say we're trusting God when life is going well, but what about when things are less than certain? That's when trust really needs to kick in and that's when we're sometimes confronted with the fact that our trust isn't as solid as we thought.

As I hid in my B&B, I reflected on the fact that it had been a particular challenging summer. One night at home I had been lying in bed when I heard a scream for help from the street. I ran down the road and found that four young people had been stabbed outside my kids' school. An argument in a nearby pub had escalated and there was blood everywhere. Another day, in the office, I was visited by a father whose son had been shot. The son had gone into a coma and had lain in a hospital bed for six months before he passed away; I couldn't even imagine how you dealt with something like that. There were increasing cases of self-harm and attempted suicide among the young people we work with and others were disclosing that their parents had been abusive. A report came out from the Children's Commissioner for England stating that 16,500 young people were at risk of sexual exploitation. The fixer in me jumps into action in these situations: I want to help people and change their painful circumstances. All I kept thinking was that I would be no help to anyone when I'd had my operation. It was agony to feel so useless. My journal had a common theme: "God, I don't understand." I couldn't see God's purposes so all I could say was "I'm trying to trust you as much as I can".

A friend of mine is a knee specialist and he asked me whether I could wait a bit longer and hang on for the knee replacement surgery, which had a comparatively short (six-week) recovery time. He wondered whether technological advancements might mean that by the time the new knees needed replacing, there would be a more permanent and less painful procedure that would help. While I was praying about this, someone came up to me at an event and said he could tell just by looking at me that I needed a knee replacement. He asked if he could take my X-rays to his doctor at a private hospital, and my heart began to soar. This could be the answer to my prayers! Perhaps there was going to be an eleventh-hour reprieve and I wouldn't have to have the operation after all!

Although I was desperate that this would prove to be a solution, I thought it was still wise to prepare for the operation while I waited to hear back. The hospital arranged for me to meet someone who had the frame so that I could get an idea of what it would be like and chat to someone in the middle of the process. Many of the men who have the frame are soldiers who have had their legs damaged by mines or in combat. I met a young guy who had been wearing his frame for eighteen months. It was his second one, as the first had become infected. This is a common problem, as the pins go through the bone and it's hard to keep the areas around the pins free from infection. It's common to have between five and eight infections during the time the frame is on. The doctors can give you antibiotics but they don't always work, and the worst-case scenario is that you have to have more surgery to remove and replace the pins. Chatting to this guy, I was beginning to get a clearer picture of what I was facing. I was still holding on to the hope that I would get a reprieve, but the news came back from the private hospital that the advice I had been given was spot on and I should go ahead. So that was it. There was nowhere left to turn, and barring a very last-minute miracle, I was about to ask a surgeon to break my leg in two places.

Every journal entry I made charted my desperate search for peace. I wanted to be like Jesus, who was able to sleep soundly despite the wind and waves tossing the boat around, but instead I felt like the disciples, who thought they were about to drown in the storm. I tried to hang on to the fact that I wasn't on my own: God was with me and would help me get through each stage of the process. I prayed he would give me a glimpse of the future; I needed his help to see beyond the next few years of physical pain, limited mobility, and endless hospital visits, so that I could find some peace and hope for my future. While I didn't hear a booming voice reassuring me that everything was going to be OK, like many people in a time like this one of the ways I knew God's love and care was through my church, friends, family, and work colleagues.

My church organized a prayer rota for me, friends gave us gifts to help us get a cleaner to reduce some of the pressure on us, and even cabinet ministers rearranged their diaries to squeeze in meetings with me before I was out of action. I was humbled and amazed by people's kindness and prayerful and practical support.

With my anxiety still high I didn't expect to sleep very much the night before the operation, but I was strangely peaceful. Usually Diane is the calmer of the two of us, but she lay awake while I quickly dozed off. Even in the morning, once we'd reached the hospital, she kept asking, "Are you sure you're OK?" I think in part I was relieved that after five years of it hovering on the horizon, the day had finally arrived. The strangest thing was that I wasn't in any pain that day, as the pain would come and go, so part of me thought, "Am I making this up? Do I even need this operation?" It was quite a surreal experience. The worst moment was when I was taken through into pre-op. I had to say goodbye to Diane and she burst into tears. I felt completely helpless as they wheeled me away from her.

I was quickly put under anaesthetic and the next thing I knew I was waking up in agony and being incredibly sick. I drifted in and out of consciousness, pressing the button on my morphine drip to try to dull the indescribable pain. The first few days were a bit of a blur. I was dizzy from the anaesthetic and sick from the morphine. The doctors tried me on a different painkiller but that made my skin painfully itchy. I don't remember much, though I do remember a guy coming in to leave me my evening meal and saying, "You look really out of it." I can't say he cheered me up much! I couldn't get up but the doctors were keen to get me moving quickly to reduce the chance of blood clots. Eventually, with the help of a Zimmer frame, I managed to make it out of bed and could see the full reality of having a huge metal frame around my leg. It was surreal to know the surgeons had severed the fibula and tibia bones in my left leg (along with the muscles around them) and to see the pins and screws that attached all the metal rings and struts to the bones. My anxiety made the pain worse and I really struggled with the fact that with visiting hours being only from 2 p.m. to 8 p.m., I was on my own with my fears for much of the time.

A few days later my dad was visiting and I started feeling hot and cold. My temperature was being monitored regularly and the nurses said it was fine and that it was just warm in the room. That didn't reassure me, as I felt freezing. My anxiety rocketed. What if I had caught something and they had missed it? I began to panic. Tears started to flow; I was sobbing and couldn't stop. I felt so out of control and was mortified, but couldn't do anything about it. Diane got the doctor to check me out and she said I was fine. She tried to reassure me that my body was simply reacting to a huge trauma and all the stress was catching up with me. I tried to bring my anxiety under control over the following days but it wasn't easy.

It felt as if God had left me. I felt lonely, isolated, and abandoned, just when I needed God the most. Then I came across this illustration in *Cross Roads* by William Paul Young,[4] pointing out that when we were young many of us believed there were monsters under the bed and that Father Christmas was real. Those things seemed like a reality but the truth is that neither exists. In our pain many of us believe that God

---

[4] William Paul Young, *Cross Roads*, Nashville, TN: FaithWorks, 2012.

has left us, but the truth is God is always there, whether we feel him or not. I needed to hang on to that truth every day even though my feelings were telling me the opposite. I had also read Greg Boyd's book *Present Perfect*, which is about knowing God's presence with you in your everyday life. He says:

> *At this moment your feet are probably being supported by the floor and your body is probably resting on a chair or sofa. When you lie down tonight, your body will be supported by your bed. Your skin is always touching some other part of the physical world, and that touch can be transformed into a little signal from the Father that he is watching over you and caring for you.*[5]

As I lay in the hospital bed, I tried to focus on that and connect with God. I found brief moments of peace but it was hard to hang on to, especially after Diane had gone home at night and I was left alone with my thoughts and worries.

Every time I had a negative thought, I felt that I needed to get it out of my head as soon as possible. But as soon as I'd got rid of one, another would pop up in its place. My friend Will van der Hart, who wrote *The Worry Book* with Rob Waller, helped me to see that trying to dismiss the negative thoughts straight away might not be the best strategy. Will suggests that when these thoughts come into our minds, we should examine them and work out what is truth and what isn't, and then we can more successfully put them out of our minds for good. This helped me to realize that it's OK to have doubts. I've often felt as if when I've

---

[5] Gregory A. Boyd, *Present Perfect*, Grand Rapids, MI: Zondervan, 2010, pages 55–56.

raised questions it's been frowned upon by other Christians, but I think it's better to voice our doubts and examine them fully rather than try to ignore them. Suppressing our doubts means living in denial. We all see the world through our own filters, which are coloured by our good and bad experiences and our unique journey in life. We may believe that the thoughts that come into our heads are right because in our world view they make sense, but we also know that others have believed they were absolutely right to start wars in God's name or to fly planes into the World Trade Center. Believing we are right doesn't *make* us right. Just because a thought appears in our mind doesn't mean that it's true. Sometimes voicing our thoughts, worries, and doubts can help us open up to a different perspective and work out what is real and what isn't.

Other people had said to me that the way to beat anxiety is to accept uncertainty, and only then will you find a measure of peace. Certainty is one of those things we all long to find and hang on to. We all know in our heads that there are few certainties in life and yet our hearts search for certainty anyway. We can make plans but we never know what tomorrow will bring. I kept asking doctors to give me definite answers about the healing process but of course they never could, because our bodies don't work like that. I wanted things to get better overnight but my process of healing was going to take months. Likewise with my anxiety: I wanted to find peace the instant I started praying for it, rather than finding it bit by bit as I journeyed with God. Will van der Hart says, "Consciously lay down your hopes for an instant fix and commit to the healing journey however long it may take."[6] That was so helpful for me. In our instant culture we want fast results and it's only when we let go of this that we can embrace the healing that needs to take place.

Praying for peace got me thinking about whether I have ever really had peace in any area of my life. When I look back, I realize there's always something I've been waiting to get out of the way before I think I will be at peace. I've thought, "When this conference is done, when that book is written, when the house is sorted, when the media attention around an incident dies down…" When, when, when. But a quiet day isn't coming! I've got four kids, so you think I would have realized this sooner! Like most parents, Diane and I barely get a moment's peace between the eldest two arguing, the third shouting to make her voice heard over the others, and the fourth enjoying nothing more than roaring like a dinosaur for no apparent reason. So there has to be more to peace than waiting for a day that's never going to come. Surely there's a way to find peace in the midst of the everyday chaos of life? The Bible talks about peace quite a lot, and some of the most famous verses on this subject come from the book of Philippians. The writer, Paul, was one of those people whose life became much more challenging after he met Jesus. Before that he had position, authority, status, and respect. He undoubtedly believed he was right to persecute the early Christians to the extreme, but that came to an abrupt end on the road to Damascus when he met Jesus. After that encounter and becoming a follower of Christ, he endured beatings, arrest, imprisonment, and shipwrecks. Unsurprisingly, then, Paul never preached that anyone who came to Jesus would

---

[6] Will van der Hart and Rob Waller, *The Worry Book*, Nottingham: IVP, 2011.

see all their problems, challenges, and frustrations disappear! He also never shied away from telling people what was going on and giving detailed accounts of his own struggles. This passage from 2 Corinthians 11 (verses 24–29) describes some of the physical, emotional, and spiritual challenges he faced:

> *Five times I received from the Jews the forty lashes minus one. Three times I was beaten with rods, once I was pelted with stones, three times I was shipwrecked, I spent a night and a day in the open sea, I have been constantly on the move. I have been in danger from rivers, in danger from bandits, in danger from my fellow Jews, in danger from Gentiles; in danger in the city, in danger in the country, in danger at sea; and in danger from false believers. I have laboured and toiled and have often gone without sleep; I have known hunger and thirst and have often gone without food; I have been cold and naked. Besides everything else, I face daily the pressure of my concern for all the churches. Who is weak, and I do not feel weak? Who is led into sin, and I do not inwardly burn?*

How could Paul, in the face of all these challenges, find peace, contentment, and even joy, rather than being consumed by anxiety and fear? He even wrote the letter to the Philippians, which explores this question, from inside a prison cell in Ephesus:

> *Rejoice in the Lord always. I will say it again: Rejoice! Let your gentleness be evident to all. The Lord is near. Do not be anxious about anything, but in every*

situation, by prayer and petition, with thanksgiving, present your requests to God. And the peace of God, which transcends all understanding, will guard your hearts and your minds in Christ Jesus...

I know what it is to be in need, and I know what it is to have plenty. I have learned the secret of being content in any and every situation, whether well fed or hungry, whether living in plenty or in want. I can do all this through him who gives me strength.

Philippians chapter 4, verses 4–7 and 12–13

Paul knew that the Philippian Christians were suffering persecution for their faith; he knew that fear and anxiety were very real experiences for them, as they had a lot to be afraid of in the first-century Roman empire. Yet he also knew that peace was possible, because he had found it in the hardest of circumstances himself. I go one of two ways when reading these passages from Philippians. Either I feel defeated because I think that Paul must have been superhuman, with a unique gift for persevering through things that no one else could have endured, and I have absolutely no hope of being like him in any way. Or I start beating myself up, remembering how much harder life is for other people, especially those who are persecuted, and I feel guilty for not trusting God more. Either way I end up feeling bad, and I'm certain that wasn't Paul's intention.

Tim Keller helpfully points out that Paul says he *has learned* to be content. He wasn't born content; it didn't come naturally to him, but he learned it. He also points out that peace is not merely an absence, it's a *presence*. It is not just an absence of fear; it's a sense of being protected by God's nearness. He says:

> *Christian peace does not start with the ousting of negative thinking. If you do that, you may simply be refusing to face how bad things are. That is one way to calm yourself – by refusing to admit the facts. But it will be short-lived peace! Christian peace doesn't start that way. It is not that you stop facing the facts, but you get a living power that comes into your life and enables you to face those realities, something that lifts you up over and through them.[7]*

I've found Paul's words so challenging as I've struggled to find peace. The funny thing is that even when we do feel peace, we can wonder why when it's not natural in the circumstances (like my being able to sleep peacefully the night before the operation that had been terrifying me for years). We can worry about the fact that we're *not* worrying! I'm slowly learning not just to take my requests to God but to leave them with him, rather than picking them up and chewing them over again and again, as I am prone to do.

For Paul, the good news is that the Philippians can be free from such anxiety. Why? Because "the Lord is near". That is important for us to know when we are in the midst of troubles: God has not left us, no matter how it may feel or appear. But Paul sees us as partners in grace with God and we have a role to play in our relationship with him if we are to receive his peace into our lives. Paul does not ask us to play mental gymnastics, or bend logic to the extremes, to

---

[7] Timothy Keller, *Walking with God through Pain and Suffering*, London: Hodder & Stoughton, 2013, page 297.

find a way of extracting divine peace. He tells us that we are called to pray to God with our requests and thanksgiving. "Prayer like that means that God's peace – not just a lack of concern for what's going on, but a deep peace in the middle of life's problems and storms – will keep guard around your hearts and mind."[8] To pray like this, to develop the spiritual discipline of prayer that can reveal God's peace, takes time before God and grows (if we allow it to) over a lifetime of relationship with a loving Father.

After my operation, as I was reflecting on the nature of peace, I remembered an old example I had heard about years ago. An artist was commissioned by a wealthy man to paint a picture showing peace. First, he painted an idyllic country scene with green fields, a blue sky, and a pretty village, but the man said it wasn't right and asked him to try again. After giving it more thought, the artist painted a mother holding a sleeping baby in her arms, but the man said that wasn't right either. Discouraged and tired, the artist sought and prayed for inspiration. An idea formed and he painted a stormy sea beating against a cliff. The sky held black rain clouds and streaks of lightning, while the waves were churning below. Where was the peace? The artist had painted a small bird, tucked safely in a nest in the rocks. The wealthy man was finally satisfied that the true nature of peace had been captured.[9] As the famous quote says: "Peace does not mean to be in a place where there is no noise, trouble, or hard work. It means to be in the midst of those things and still be calm in your heart."

---

[8] N. T. Wright, *Paul for Everyone – The Prison Letters*, London: SPCK/Louisville, KY: Westminster John Knox, 2002, page 131.

[9] http://www.sermoncentral.com/sermons/peace-tim-zingale-sermon-on-miracles-of-jesus-92288.asp

Andy's Story

Andy is one of life's completely unassuming guys, quietly and generously giving and serving in whatever ways he can. He has a disability that you'll read about below but he has never let that stop him from pursuing his dreams. I've seen him campaigning from door to door, knowing the physical toll that takes on him, but he refuses to be defined by his disability. Through various circumstances over the years he has had every reason to be down, but instead he's always upbeat. Every time we've met for coffee I've come away excited after hearing what God is doing in his life, and feeling uplifted in my faith. Some people like to talk about themselves a lot while others, like Andy, prefer to focus on Jesus. This is his story of knowing God in the midst of life's pain and suffering.

> My first clear memory is of hearing a doctor tell my mum and dad that I would never walk. That same day I heard an audible voice say, "Stick with me and you will walk." I was five years old and thought it was an ordinary thing to hear God's voice! I was born in 1970 and as there were no scans then my mother had no idea she was pregnant with twins. She went into labour seven weeks early and my brother was born weighing just 4lb, while I was 3lb 14oz. As they weren't expecting me I remained in the womb for too long and was starved of oxygen, meaning I was

born with cerebral palsy. My brother and I were christened on that same day as the doctors didn't think either of us would survive the night.

Five years after the doctors told me I wouldn't walk, I did! I think overcoming the odds from such a young age has meant that every time someone tells me I can't do something it just makes me want to try to prove them wrong. The cerebral palsy does affect the way that I walk, though, and that has meant people have stared at me, spat at me, and laughed at me as I've walked down the street. I was taught that it was their problem and not mine so I shrugged it off and said I didn't care. It's only in more recent years that God has shown me how much that rejection affected me. My mum and dad were great and sent me to a mainstream school, not wanting me to miss out on anything. It was brilliant having a twin brother, as we could do everything together. I never really asked "Why me?" about my disability; I've always tried to look at the positives of it. For example, when something is harder for you, such as getting down steps without a handrail, you have to find a way around it, meaning that creative problem-solving becomes second nature.

Although I heard God's voice when I was a child, I didn't become a Christian until I was twenty-eight. I had gone on an Alpha course because I wanted to prove Christians wrong but when I finished the last evening I sat in my car on a snowy winter's night and said, "God, if you're there, you'd better show me." I immediately burst into tears, which was something I rarely did. Because I'd been teased and taunted so much as a child I hardly ever allowed myself to cry. Right there in the car, the first thing God said to me was, "I love you, so it doesn't matter what anyone else thinks of you." Those words were the start of a healing journey for me and I've held on to them through the years since.

Two weeks after committing my life to Jesus, I started working at a Christian youth club in Croydon, South London. When I hit thirty, I left my job as a council policy officer to move onto an estate in Croydon to work with the church there. We asked the community what they wanted and started running kids clubs, social events for retired people, parenting courses, and a Christians Against Poverty (CAP) money programme. Four years later one of the young people we were working with was stabbed to death. It was incredibly painful for everyone in the community who knew him. All I kept asking God was, what was the point? Why was I there if I couldn't stop these kids from getting hurt? I cried for twenty-four hours, desperately confused. God said to me, "My glory will be seen in this situation," and that was the only thing that helped me get up and carry on.

The more time I spent with the young people, the more I realized that the system wasn't working for them, and I wanted to get up the policy ladder to affect things at a higher level. I started working with the Centre for Social Justice on their "Breakthrough Britain" report looking at ways to tackle poverty. I became interested in politics and in the 2010 general election I stood to be MP for Camberwell and Peckham, the most deprived constituency in England. I didn't get elected but shortly afterwards went back to Croydon to set up a charity called Ment4 with a friend, offering intensive mentoring for teenagers with behavioural challenges. It was hard work but I loved it.

Andy's Story

After the election I realized that my mobility was reduced and I had less energy than before. For about a year, when I spent time with God I felt him reminding me that I could have died on the day that I was born. I felt challenged to be grateful for all the years that I'd had and all the things I'd been able to do. I wasn't sure why he was telling me this repeatedly but I knew I had been blessed to have the life that I'd had. I wondered if I was going to become even less mobile. People prayed for my healing, which I've never discouraged, but nothing changed. I've always felt a certain peace knowing that I'll get a new body in heaven. I can't wait for that but I've made my peace with my earthly body too.

I noticed I was losing a bit of weight and was pleased about that, but then I started getting some stomach problems. The doctors diagnosed me with IBS and gallstones and things got gradually worse. By February 2013 I couldn't eat without throwing up. The doctor sent me to A&E and twenty-four hours after a CT scan was done I was told I had Stage Two bowel cancer. In a strange way I wasn't surprised; it made sense after what God had been saying to me about being grateful for the life I'd lived so far. I was amazed that he had prepared me for this news and that meant I knew his presence in the situation straight away. I was operated on immediately and it was supposed to be a straightforward procedure that would leave me able to go home in a week. Unfortunately there was a leak in my bowel when they sewed me back together, and as a result I had to spend two months in hospital. In total I didn't eat for fifty-one days and for several weeks was fed through a tube directly into my bloodstream. Sometimes it felt as if the doctors were at a loss to know how to treat me and what to do about the leak. At one point they said they were going to have to operate again and I was desperate that they didn't. I couldn't face the trauma of another operation and it felt so hard that the treatment was going backwards when I really needed it to go forwards. I asked my church to pray for me and within a few days the leak had stopped of its own accord and the doctors said I wouldn't need any more surgery! It opened my eyes to the power of prayer. There were a couple of nights in hospital when I could feel the anxiety creeping up on me, but I prayed for peace and had an amazing sense of God's presence calming me. I saw God at work in other ways too. One night a friend of mine who was addicted to cocaine came to visit me. I had been praying for his salvation for years, but every time I'd tried to talk to him about God he'd shut the conversation down. This time, however, he told me he'd had a dream in which he was sitting at my feet in tears. We talked about it and he said he wanted to give his life to Jesus, so I led him through the prayer of commitment there in my hospital bed! I hadn't seen him for two months and it was another reminder to me that God doesn't need me to fulfil his purposes.

When I could eat again I tried some cornflakes, and after eight weeks without tasting a single thing, they were like little pieces of heaven. How many times in my life had I eaten cornflakes and taken them for granted? Suddenly they were the best thing in the world. It's amazing how losing something can make us appreciate it more. When I was strong enough to leave that hospital I had to have six months of chemotherapy at the Royal Marsden Hospital. I'd have the treatment every three weeks and for four days afterwards I wouldn't be able to do anything. My brain would be foggy and I had no energy to talk or to move. Even watching TV was too difficult. The chemo tablets I had to take upset my stomach too, but at least for a few

Andy's Story

weeks I was able to function before I had to have the next round of treatment.

When you're ill your world contracts very quickly. Until then my diary had always been full and I was constantly busy; suddenly life became so limited that even getting out of bed and sitting in a chair for half an hour was a big deal. It was a strange situation to learn to connect with God. Some nights I didn't think I had the energy to carry on living. When you're facing death, surrender to God takes on a whole new form. I laid everything down before him. When you can't do anything, you have to let go of the need to perform. This was the beginning of a journey for me and I have a long way to go, but I know I need to let go of the need to "do" in order to be of value. I used to be a real planner too, always looking to the future and asking what's next, but I learned to live just one day at a time.

Facing your own mortality also hones what's really important. It didn't matter that I hadn't been able to fulfil my ambition to be an MP; all I cared about were my family and the young people I'd been mentoring for years. I knew that if I died my family would grieve, but they would have each other, which would ultimately see them through. The guys I mentored, on the other hand, didn't have the support they needed and I wanted to change that in case my treatment was unsuccessful. When it came down to life and death, the only thing that mattered was a handful of relationships.

After I had finished the chemo my mobility dropped about 80 per cent, but because I've always had difficulty walking people didn't really notice. Everyone thought I was recovered but I was actually still far from it. They began asking me to do things and everything in me wanted to say yes, but I knew I couldn't always manage it. Sometimes I had to ask others to help me, which I found really difficult. During that time I felt that God was telling me to put everything down. I love to be doing things and helping people so I found that very challenging. I could see that I needed some time to recover but I couldn't bear the thought of it being open-ended, so I agreed to take a month off and went to Devon to relax and rest. My friend Pete continued to run Ment4 and he kept my part-time job open for me when I returned. As I was thinking about returning to work I saw an advert for another part-time job for a charity in Croydon that worked with retired people. I decided to push the door to see what happened, and I got the job! This is the role I'm currently in and I manage our 300 volunteers and 300 clients. A few months ago I was elected as a local councillor in Croydon and I'm mentoring some of the young guys I've known for a while. I'm still learning about being kind to myself; looking back, I suspect God wanted me to put things down for longer than I did. He's still challenging me to balance my activism with rest. It takes a long time to change but I cling on to the fact that we are being changed into God's image from one degree of glory to another (2 Corinthians 3:18). People say, "It's good to see you back to normal," but the truth is I don't feel like my old self and am still struggling to find a "new normal" and a "new self". When I was in my hospital bed, life was very simple. I couldn't move around easily and I had only God to rely on, so I could spend my days talking to him without feeling guilty about a list of things I should be doing. Then, as you recover, your life starts to get busy again, the "to do" list starts to grow, and things become complicated once more. I now find myself craving those "simple" times with God. I don't think I have got the balance right yet, but I am still searching for it.

People have asked me a lot about suffering and one thing I know is that each of us suffers in our own way. I think the question is whether we will let it master us or whether we will allow God to use it to build perseverance, character, and hope in us. I believe we should be honest about the times we're hurting but that we should try to look for God's hope beyond the hurt. I do still struggle with anxiety but I'm trying to live in the present rather than worrying about tomorrow. Before the cancer I had a five-year plan for my life. Now I try to take things more slowly and lay things before God, asking him what he wants me to do and how he wants me to do it. There's a 30 per cent chance the cancer will come back so I have to have regular check-ups, and each time I have to prepare myself for potential bad news. Living with that awareness means I try to live day by day, aiming to enjoy life in the present because the future is uncertain. Some Christians said to me, "It's not your time," about the cancer, but I felt the challenge that if the cancer was terminal, I wanted to die well. I had hope that even while I was lying in a hospital bed, I could still try to inspire people about who God is. We can still have an impact for God's kingdom right up to our death. When I felt particularly anxious one time, I prayed and felt God say, "What's the worst that could happen?" I thought about it and realized that, even if I died, God was still in control. Dying simply means I get to go to the best party in the world earlier than I was expecting, and that's really not such a bad prospect.

Chapter 3

Rethinking Courage

Eight days after the operation, I had to have some X-rays taken to check that the bones were welding back together correctly. The results were good and the consultants said I could leave hospital that day, which was a huge surprise, as we'd been told I would have to stay in for two more days. So suddenly Diane was rushing around trying to get the house ready for my arrival and I found myself being driven home in an ambulance. I was carried inside on a stretcher and transferred onto the sofa; it felt good to have a change of scenery and be able to look out of a window instead of at a stark wall. But, although I was back in familiar surroundings, everything was different. I was still in lots of pain and couldn't push myself up from the sofa, so I couldn't get up without help. I knew the kids would be arriving home from school shortly and while I was desperate to see them, my overriding feeling was one of fear. Caleb was still far too small to understand what was going on and I was petrified he would try to haul himself up on my leg frame, pulling on all the pins in my legs. Just the thought of it made me feel sick. Guilt weighed heavily that I wasn't purely excited to see them when they walked through the door, but every time they came near I tensed, waiting for the jostles and jolts that would cause me agony.

We'd decided not to make up a bed for me downstairs as we wanted to try to keep life as normal as possible. The hospital had helped me practise moving up and down stairs with the frame on, but of course it's a whole different story practising with medical staff, in a building designed for people who have mobility problems, rather than in your own home. We didn't have double banisters for me to be able to hold on to for a start, and at one point where the stairs turned a corner, there was no banister at all. My heart was pounding and my hands were shaking; I didn't know if I could keep my balance or whether I was about to go crashing down to the bottom. My mum tried to help me, and had to catch me a couple of times when I missed a step, but by the time I reached the top of the staircase I was an absolute wreck. I couldn't believe that such a simple task, which most of us do unthinkingly multiple times a day, had taken everything I had. I began to sob and then to shout, "I can't do it! I can't get through this!" I had nothing left and yet I knew I was just at the beginning of a very long ordeal.

Our parents kindly took our kids for the weekend to give us some more time to adjust, but the roller coaster continued as we tried to work out what life was going to look like for the next season. I spent a lot of time lying on the sofa trying to find a good position, but couldn't get comfortable. I had eight pillows supporting me but my back still really hurt. I tried to find things to distract me but when you can't move and you're in pain, it's hard to focus on anything else. Every time I tried to do something it would take me ten times as long as it normally did, and I couldn't help but get frustrated.

The worst part of the day was when Diane had to do the alterations. There were six struts between the top and middle ring of the frame, and another six between the middle and bottom ring. They were numbered and colour-coded. When the frame is put on, they try to set the leg as straight as humanly possible. The measurements are fed into a computer, which then figures out the ultimate measurements each strut should be at for a perfectly straight leg. This final result is then broken down into daily measurement changes and printed out onto a prescription. Diane had to read the prescription daily and adjust all the required pins for that day. She was literally moving my leg around inside. This didn't hurt immediately but twenty minutes afterwards, the pain would kick in. It was unbearable and I just had to lie there and wait for it to pass.

Before the operation I had done some research on courage, knowing I was going to need a huge amount of it to see me through. My previous images of courage had been the heroic acts of those on the battlefield, or the Hollywood image of the boxer who refuses to go down and ends up winning in the final round. But now, lying on the sofa, completely drained, those images seemed to offer little solace or encouragement. I felt fearful, guilty, and unable to cope with the pain – exhausted, helpless, and lonely. I had a strong urge to withdraw and hide; I didn't want people to see me like that. I didn't feel that I could relate to the notions of courage I once had, but I found a far greater connection to this quote from Mary Anne Radmacher: "Courage does not always roar. Sometimes it's the quiet voice at the end of the day saying, 'I will try again tomorrow.'"

I was also inspired by the work of Brené Brown, a research professor who has spent more than ten years studying vulnerability and courage. I started to realize that courage is about allowing yourself to be vulnerable. As she puts it, "Courage starts with showing up and letting ourselves be seen".[10] She also helped me understand the real meaning of the word "courage":

> *Courage is a heart word. The root of the word courage is cor – the Latin word for heart. In one of its earliest forms, the word courage meant "To speak one's mind by telling all one's heart."… Today, we typically associate courage with heroic and brave deeds. But in my opinion, this definition fails to recognize the inner strength and level of commitment required for us to actually speak honestly and openly about who we are and about our experiences – good and bad. Speaking from our hearts is what I think of as "ordinary courage."*[11]

When Brené was first asked to do a TED talk (www.ted.com) she thought it would be heard by about 500 people. Over 6 million watched it. The topic of vulnerability caught people's imagination and tapped into something many of us haven't wanted to face. She talked about how we avoid vulnerability, running from it as best we can, and when we find ourselves feeling vulnerable, we do all we can to numb it. Of course we can't outrun something that is so fundamental to life, and so

---

[10] http://www.goodreads.com/quotes/625801-courage-starts-with-showing-up-and-letting-ourselves-be-seen

[11] https://www.goodreads.com/quotes/737201-courage-is-a-heart-word-the-root-of-the-word

we find ourselves in debt, obese, and dealing with addictions. And we can't selectively numb either; if we numb the bad feelings, we're inevitably numbing the good ones too – and where does that leave us? As Brené says, it takes true courage for us to allow others to see who we truly are.

In a recent seminar, I got the group to carry out an exercise that Brené had tried, and I asked them to finish the sentence "Vulnerability is…". These are some of their answers:

- Letting other people and God see your heart
- Living how God created you to live, not how your friends want you to live
- Taking a step in faith, without knowing where it will lead
- Being the one to stand up for prayer when no one around you has stood up
- Trusting God
- Allowing yourself to face the pain of abuse and refusing to let it define your future
- When you let people see the real you, the person behind all the barriers
- Allowing others to share your burdens with you
- Admitting to self-harming to your closest friends and family
- Not being afraid of having an opinion
- Standing by your brother's bed having been told he is going to die, yet believing God has the power to heal, so hoping and praying for that healing

- Letting people see you cry
- Looking in the mirror and not trying to change what you see.

I'm not sure how you feel reading that list, but I was amazed at the level of bravery in the answers. These things don't strike me as weak in any way. Vulnerable? Yes. Weak? Not in the least. They show an admirable level of strength, courage, and determination.

My operation meant that I went from being very independent and setting impossibly high standards for myself to realizing that I had to let others help me. For the first few weeks I needed help with everything – even the simplest of tasks – and I found it so frustrating. In Christian circles we often say that our identity lies not in what we do but in who we are. This is an easy thing to say from a pulpit (often by many of us who have full-time jobs), but it's much harder to hold on to that truth when what we do is taken away. Many of us derive a measure of worth, rightly or wrongly, from what we do. I have worked with many young people over the years who have been long-term unemployed and I've seen how much it affects someone's self-worth when they have no job at all. Many of us don't realize how much of our sense of personal value is tied up in our job until we're not able to work for some reason.

For the first couple of weeks after the operation I would find myself bursting into tears, seemingly for no reason. A large part of it was that I couldn't stand not feeling useful. My whole identity was being shaken, and in some ways still is. The days of having back-to-back meetings at work and looking after the kids after school before rushing out to an event in the evening had vanished; instead, my aims became much simpler. I would set myself such tiny goals of walking to the first tree from our house and then the next day of trying to make it to the second one. I didn't feel courageous; I felt weak and small. These didn't feel like the goals of a grown man but of a young child who is learning to walk. But even though part of me wanted to hide away, I knew I needed to share what I was going through. I'd spoken about my operation in public before it happened and many people had been kind and supportive, praying for me during the operation and as I recovered. I wanted to share some of the things I was dealing with, partly as a way of helping me process what was going on, and partly in order to practise some of the courage of vulnerability by letting people see the real me. I hoped that at some point I would emerge from this season and be able to share the things I had seen God do, but I wanted to discuss what was going on while I was still feeling weak and confused, so that people could know the full picture. As I wasn't able to do any public speaking, I decided to communicate through writing a blog. I wrote the first one, called "When faith gets shaken", and was amazed by the response. I had comments and emails from people who had been through so much more than I have, many on a journey with cancer and having chemo or seeing loved ones face some incredible challenges. There was a son looking after an elderly parent who had dementia, and a thirty-seven-year-old who had leukemia, a number of people who had panic disorders, a gentleman who had had open heart surgery and whose wife had been diagnosed with lupus. Some just commented on how much they appreciated my vulnerability and honesty. Sharing my own confusion and weakness opened the door for others to do the same.

I commented to my pastor that when someone is healed, the first thing we want to do in the church is bring them to the front, give them a microphone, and let them give their testimony to encourage the congregation and increase their faith. But, as I knew from experience, sometimes we also need to hear from those who haven't yet been healed so we can encourage one another to keep going in our vulnerability. We have to make space for our weakness. Author Keith Miller said:

> *Our churches are filled with people who outwardly look contented and at peace but inwardly are crying out for someone to love them… just as they are – confused, frustrated, often frightened, guilty and often unable to communicate with their own families. But the other people in the church look so happy and contented that one seldom has the courage to admit his own deep needs before such a self-sufficient group as the average church meeting appears to be.*[12]

Jesus gave us the ultimate examples of this vulnerability from his birth through to his death. He allowed himself to be born in a violent land recovering from civil wars, in a place that was still in turmoil. He entrusted himself to a young couple who would soon become refugees on the run in Africa. He was as helpless and vulnerable as any baby, fully dependent on other people to take care of him, and unable to even

---

[12] Keith Miller, as quoted in Howard Snyder, *The Problem of Wineskins*, Downers Grove, MI: InterVarsity Press, 1975, page 90.

control his own bladder. And at the end of his earthly life he made himself intensely vulnerable again, placing his body into the hands of those who wished him harm, and facing the torture ahead with great courage.

Paul modelled his life on Jesus and neither shied away from speaking from their hearts, whether things were good or bad (such as in 2 Corinthians 1:8–11). Jesus told us that the most important things we can ever do are to love God and to love other people (Mark 12:30–31), and those were the two things he did that strengthened him to complete what God had called him to do. Paul knew that life is filled with difficulties, disappointment, and opposition, and he knew that only by continuing to love God and each other would we have the strength, like Jesus, to finish the race marked out for us. Loving God and people takes courage; it means being open and honest and making ourselves vulnerable, with no guarantee of how people will respond. We can't have a real, loving, relationship with someone with whom we're not prepared to be open, honest, and vulnerable. And when we do find the courage to be like that, we begin to see a new depth in our relationships with people and with God. Contrary to popular belief and the prevailing culture of the day, the strongest relationships are most often forged in the heat of difficulty and in confessing our weaknesses. It is in the fellowship created by such relationships that strength begins to emerge that will see us all through to completing God's work in us and the mission God has for us on earth. We share a common humanity. Every single one of us has times of feeling weak, fearful, confused, ashamed, miserable, anxious, or angry, and it's often as we share those feelings that others really feel they can connect with us, as they can relate to what we're going through. Sometimes we might feel that we have to look as though we've got it all sorted in front of people who don't know Jesus, as we think that will make us better witnesses, but I wonder if it's when we share our weakness that they start to see us as fully rounded humans, not as mystical beings who pretend to be perfect. The messages I'd had in response to my blog inspired me with their courage and dignity. It's so easy to fall into the trap of feeling that you're the only one going through something painful and to think that no one else will understand. But when we're honest, we give other people permission to be honest too. Together we realize we are part of a community that doesn't have all the answers, but can take hold of each other's hands and say, "Let's try again tomorrow."

Chapter 4

Standing Stubbornly Nowhere

One thing I hadn't expected about my recovery was that it would be so hard to concentrate. So many people had commented that having all that time in which I was forced to sit down would give me plenty of opportunity to catch up on some DVD box sets and books, and you might think I would have raced through them. Instead, I would start a book and find my mind wandering. I would try to watch a series such as *24*, which I usually love, but find the violence was too much and have to turn it off. I tried to do some work from home but couldn't focus on emails or find the energy to deal with them. I found it hard not being able to help around the house, especially as I could see that Diane was growing increasingly tired as a result of the extra pressures falling on her shoulders. I would have given anything to be able to be useful but I wasn't even able to help clear the plates after dinner, let alone take my share of the burden when it came to looking after the kids and running a busy household. Caleb would cry and I couldn't get to him or pick him up. He became wary of me, and it was hard to get him even to sit next to me so that I could read him a story. He was too young to understand why I wasn't the dad he knew, why I couldn't get down on the floor to play with him, or let him climb over me as he used to. I couldn't bear to see the confusion on his face and it hurt so much that I couldn't just scoop him up and make it better.

I was thankful for friends from XLP who came to visit and to update me on things that were happening. There was a strange thing, though: I'd hear about a fundraising event or prayer meeting that had gone smoothly and I'd feel proud of the team and excited that things were going well. Then I'd get this niggling fear that things were going so well without me that maybe they didn't need me… People asked me what I missed most: was it the young people? The team? Speaking in churches? Doing press interviews? What I think it boiled down to was that I missed feeling useful and being able to contribute. I felt as if I was sitting on the bench, on the sidelines of life, while everyone else was getting stuck in and playing the game in front of me.

I didn't want to start getting a victim mentality and being trapped in a cycle of "poor me", but equally I knew I couldn't (and shouldn't) paint on a smile and pretend everything was OK. The physical challenges were tough but the hardest thing was feeling so numb spiritually. I kept thinking about all the people who had told me that they'd known God most closely in their times of suffering. I felt as if my body and spirit were taking a daily beating, and yet I had no sense of God's presence. In the darkest moments I wondered if God had left me. I knew it wasn't just the operation that was making me feel so low. It was an accumulation of years of working with broken people in desperate situations, years of limping on, worrying about my own health and dealing with health problems in the family.

I felt guilty about the impact it was all having on Diane (which she will talk about in detail in Chapter 7), and on the rest of the family. The cumulative impact had caught up with me and weighed heavily on my heart and mind. My prayers were short and desperate: "Please say something, God. *Anything*" seemed to be the theme. It's easy to presume that everyone else is praying and enjoying the glorious nearness of God and we're the only one on the outside, so I took comfort in some of my heroes of the faith whose struggles seemed all too familiar to me. Henri Nouwen is one of those heroes, having written a number of books that have influenced me greatly. Nouwen was a priest, professor, pastor, and author who wrote over forty books on the spiritual life, which have been translated into over twenty-two languages. In 1995, a year before his death, he wrote about prayer, but rather than describing an amazing intimacy with his creator, as you might expect from this spiritual giant, he described a painful lack. He said that he didn't enjoy prayer and didn't do it often, feeling as though his prayers were "dead as a rock". Though he had learned much about prayer through painstaking research, he said he felt few emotions when praying:

> *Whereas for a long time the Spirit acted so clearly through my flesh, now I feel nothing. I have lived with the expectation that prayer would be easier as I grow older and older and close to death. But the opposite seems to be happening. The words darkness and dryness seem to best describe my prayer today.*[13]

---

[13] Henri Nouwen, *Sabbatical Journey*, New York: The Crossroad Publishing Company, 1998, pages 5–6; also quoted in Philip Yancey, *Reaching for the Invisible God*, Grand Rapids, MI: Zondervan, 2000, page 186.

I think it was honesty such as this that attracted people to Nouwen's books; we want to know that we're not alone when we're struggling. But the picture he painted wasn't entirely bleak. He also said:

> *Are the darkness and dryness of my prayer signs of God's absence, or are the signs of presence deeper and wider than the senses can contain? Is the death of my prayer the end of my intimacy with God or the beginning of a new communion, beyond words, emotions and bodily sensations?*[14]

In the midst of the darkness, he found light. He had hope that God was still with him and that no matter what was happening, it could lead him to a greater intimacy with his heavenly Father. Another hero of mine, Mother Teresa, also experienced a similarly dark season. You would think that with the amazing ways she served God through her work in the slums she must have had a hotline to him, but she said that a year after commencing her missionary activities her spirit felt as though it was in darkness and her prayers seemed empty. She continued to pour herself into her work but was of course incredibly pained at losing her intimacy with Jesus. Finally, a wise priest encouraged her to write down her feelings and describe her emptiness and confusion.

One of the most respected spiritual leaders of our times said she was at a point when she struggled to pray and had no faith. Interestingly, when these journals were found, after her death, some didn't think they should be published. This private spiritual anguish didn't seem to fit with the saintly

---

[14] Nouwen, quoted in *The Heart of Henri Nouwen*, New York: The Crossroad Publishing Company, 2003, page 96.

woman the world thought it knew. Ultimately the Vatican said they should be published as they reveal the very nature of faith, and these words have gone on to provide comfort to many who recognize their own struggles as they read Mother Teresa's.

I was inspired by the fact that Mother Teresa kept going; I was desperate to hang on to God no matter what. I started writing short prayers, which often consisted of "God, why the distance?!" God felt so far away and yet, because I knew in my head that he is loving and kind, I was sure he was trying to whisper to me. As I write this, it's tempting to try to find answers to what was going on, but the reality was that I had none then, and I still don't have any now. All I could do was cling to the truth that although it didn't feel as if God was with me, I knew that he was.

As I tried to pass the monotonous days at home I finally found a TV programme I could concentrate on: *Planet Earth* shown on the BBC. There was an episode all about deserts and I thought it would be deathly boring, presuming that nothing can live in such an unforgiving habitat. The first words David Attenborough spoke grabbed my attention: "There isn't a desert in the world that doesn't have life in it." Christians quite often talk about the times when we don't know God's presence as "desert times". These seasons feel lonely, dry, and barren but, as David Attenborough reminded me, that doesn't mean there isn't growth and life. We're so led by what we see, looking for growth on the surface and obvious signs of God's presence, that sometimes we miss what he is doing below the surface. I knew I was feeling lonely and dry but I knew there was truth in the idea that there is life in the desert even if it isn't obvious. Maybe, just maybe, God would use this season to develop a deeper trust and a stronger friendship between us.

I started to think about the people we read of in the Bible who spent time in the desert. Moses spent much of his life working in the desert as a shepherd, and it was there that he had his famous encounter with God by the burning bush. After his dramatic encounters with Pharaoh and eventually leading God's people out of Egypt, Moses found himself back in the desert again. This time he saw God provide food and water for his people in miraculous ways and learned a humble dependence on God. The desert place often seems to be the one where we begin to depend on God in a whole new way, aware of our own inadequacies. In church we often talk about how Jesus said "apart from me you can do nothing" (John 15:5), but that doesn't mean that God hasn't given us natural gifts that we can use to achieve many things. I think the difference is that God doesn't want us to rely on these gifts, but instead to rely on him. Most of us struggle with that, and in fact it has been the struggle of God's people through the ages. Even as Moses was meeting God face to face in the desert, the people were getting restless. By the time Moses had got back down the mountain they had persuaded Aaron to make them a golden calf; they didn't know what had happened to Moses, and out of fear and a desire to take control, they had made an idol rather than wait for God (Exodus 32). Most of us can probably relate to that. Sometimes when God asks us to wait we find the pressure too much and decide we had better take things into our own hands. The Israelites got Aaron to make the calf quickly to satisfy their immediate need for something to worship. In comparison, when God told them to build a tabernacle (the place where he would dwell) so they could come to worship him there, there was nothing quick about it. God asked the people to bring different items as they felt led (Exodus 25:1–9, 35:4 – 36:7) and gave exact instructions for how it was to look. God longed to travel with his people as they took on the painstaking preparations for his sanctuary; they just wanted a quick result. Moses, on the other hand, found a real intimacy with God in the desert. He spoke face to face with God "as a man speaks with his friend" (Exodus 33:11), and God said, "I am pleased with you and I know you by name" (verse 17).

Of course, Jesus too spent forty days in a desert. It was just after his baptism, which you would think would be the perfect time for him to get on with some miracles so that people would know that his ministry had started. Instead, he spent forty days being tested and tempted. It sounds harrowing, however he didn't return burned out and in need of a break but full of the power of the Holy Spirit and ready to begin his ministry. The desert was not just a necessary but an absolutely essential part of his life. While each of these people had a very different reason for being in the desert, the desert experience was a vital opportunity for them to develop a deeper dependence on God.

I tried to focus on these things and took comfort from seeing through the Bible that even though I felt as if I was in a desert, it didn't mean that God had left me. But while it helped to a certain degree, I still felt pretty much the same. Day by day it was just me, in constant pain from my leg and with additional pain in my back from the weight of the frame, dealing with symptoms of IBS and eczema brought on by stress, not sleeping well, and feeling helpless as I couldn't even stand up alone. Diane and I both felt at a loss as to how to cope. At one particularly bleak moment she stepped out of the room to take a minute on her own to cry out to God. She told him it was too hard and that she couldn't do it any more. As she prayed she saw a picture of a tunnel and immediately thought of the old adage "the light at the end of the tunnel". But as she looked she couldn't see any light in the distance; the tunnel seemed too long. As she looked again she saw that the light was around her, at the *start* of the tunnel, not the end. In that second, she knew God had given her our survival strategy to get us through the difficult months ahead: we had to be fully present in the moment. We couldn't look at how life might be in a day, a week, a month, or a year; if we looked ahead waiting for the light, we'd miss seeing that it was with us right where we stood.

It's a challenge, isn't it? So much of our time is spent thinking about the next thing or waiting for what's ahead that we miss out on what's right in front of us. Many of us long to be more present in each moment but find ourselves grabbing our phones to send a work email about a meeting the next day when we could be reading a story to our kids, flicking on the TV guide to see what's coming up before the programme we're watching has even finished, letting our minds wander from the conversation we're having because we're thinking about the things on our to-do list. I know I'm often guilty of being physically present while my mind is miles away. We've also taken multitasking to a whole new level thanks to smartphones, laptops, and tablets. Watching TV is no longer enough; we have to be tweeting about it, while checking the news and tomorrow's weather and responding to every email and text that comes in. A recent study[15] concluded that "There is no such thing as true multi-tasking; our brains are yet to evolve the capacity to actually perform two completely different cognitive processes simultaneously. Mental tasks that feel like they are being done in parallel actually involve rapid switching between the two." Their studies showed that during a half-hour period of watching TV, people will switch between two screens on average 120 times. That's about four times per minute, or once every fifteen seconds. No matter what we're doing, it seems we also feel the need to check our smartphones once every six and a half minutes. How often are we actually fully present in the moment? And what is it that drives us to keep pushing on to the next thing without pausing to finish the current one? Brennan Manning writes, "To stand stubbornly in nowhere, rejecting the restlessness that urges us to move on, silencing the voices that entice us into tomorrow… is an act of unflappable trust in the presence of God."[16] That floors me. When I've done a talk, given a press interview, or had a sensitive conversation with someone, I'll inevitably chew it over afterwards, going over it and thinking through everything I could have done differently. It's like having the nastiest *X Factor* judge living in my head, pouncing on everything I've done wrong and all the ways I could improve. But, as I said earlier, I also waste time thinking about the future and holding out for that perfect moment when life will become easy. In moderation it's good to both reflect on the past and plan for the future, but if we spend most of our time in either the past

---

[15] By Adrian Webster and Dr Jack Lewis, as found in their book *Sort Your Brain Out: Boost Your Performance, Manage Stress and Achieve More*, Chicester: Capstone, 2014.

[16] Brennan Manning, *Ruthless Trust*, Harper San Francisco, 2002, page 153.

or the future, we miss out on everything that's happening today. When we stop and live in the moment, we're putting everything else in God's capable hands and trusting in him.

When the late Hollywood film director John Frankenheimer was asked if he got nervous before shooting an 80-million-dollar movie with the world's megastars, he said, "The most important thing for me as a human being and a movie director is to give undivided presence to the present. The past is something I can't do anything about. The future is terrifying because none of this ends well, as we know. So you have to stay right here, right now."[17] Bishop John Pritchard picks up this theme in his excellent book *God Lost and Found*. He suggests that we may in fact rush past the God we say we seek, instead of engaging with him in the moment. So often we look for God in the big and spectacular, waiting for the highs of the big conferences and the extraordinary moments of life, rather than becoming more aware of him in the everyday and mundane areas of our life. Pritchard writes:[18]

> *Musicians are fond of saying that the space between the notes is as important as the notes themselves. In the dryness and the waiting we become less arrogant and more humble, less certain and more searching, less selfish and more obedient. Above all we may discover new things about the location of God.*

God is always with us, whether we recognize it or not. In Genesis 28:12–15 we read about Jacob's dream of a stairway

---

[17] *Newsweek*, 27 April 1998, page 60.
[18] John Pritchard, *God Lost and Found*, London: SPCK, 2011, page 11.

that reaches from earth to heaven. He saw the angels of God going up and down this stairway and God spoke to him through the dream. When he woke up, Jacob said, "Surely the Lord is in this place, and I was not aware of it" (verse 16). How often do we go about our lives, sidetracked by all sorts of things, looking and longing for God, and completely unaware that he's right there with us as we go about our everyday tasks? Stopping is uncomfortable, though. Most of us don't do it unless we're forced to, and even though we know we probably should slow down, it feels so countercultural that we keep hurrying along. I noticed that while I was forced to stop, the lives of my friends were carrying on at full speed as normal. For the first few weeks after the operation there was always someone coming to visit, giving me a call, or sending me a text. As the weeks went on, it all dropped off. Occasionally there would be a text or a call saying, "Sorry I've not been round; things are so busy." In truth, I couldn't blame anyone for that because I could recognize that I would have done the same. When someone first needs help it's easy to swing into action and rescue mode. But when they need help for a prolonged period, it's hard to fit it into life's busy schedule. People say that children spell love "T-I-M-E". Maybe we all do. People are always more important than anything else. My mum is a long-serving hospice nurse, and when people are coming to the end of their life she's seen time and time again that they're not interested in their bank account or accomplishments; they just want to be with the people they love. We've all heard stories of people seemingly hanging on to life despite all the odds, just waiting for those they love to get to their bedside so they can see them one last time. Those moments together are so precious, and yet how often in everyday life do we waste such opportunities to be with those we love? I knew I wanted to be fully present with my family and with God despite my feelings. My prayer life became more honest and I started to let go of the notion that I should be experiencing the glory of God every time I prayed. I tried to focus on the fact that God was with me despite my complete lack of awareness of his presence. I was determined not to let bitterness and confusion stop me praying because deep down, despite everything, I still had this longing to connect with God. I tried to focus on the small rays of light that were with me each day, rather than looking for the end of the tunnel, waiting for a bright light shining there. Every time I had a bad day, Diane would remind me that all we can do is take one day at a time.

Liza's Story

Liza and I first wrote together in 2007 and this is now our fourth book. Writing a book can be a very vulnerable experience, especially a book like this one that is so personal, so you need to be able to trust the person you are working with absolutely. I trust Liza completely – not just for her amazing ability to write, but because of her character and integrity. She is so easy to work with and it helps that she has the ability to laugh when we're under pressure from tight deadlines! I wanted her to tell some of her story of how faith can get shaken when life doesn't work out in the ways that you want it to and your dreams aren't being fulfilled.

> When I was a teenager I had a postcard that said, "Don't let your fears stand in the way of your dreams." I stuck it on my wall and I've kept it ever since, as something about it spoke to me. The funny thing is that for years I let my fears stand in the way of my dreams without even realizing it. When I felt that God was calling me out of my safe public relations job and into the unknown world of writing fiction, I wasn't sure I'd heard him right. I'd always been a "play it safe" kind of person; I didn't like taking risks and I only really liked to try something new if there was a decent chance I could do it well. I certainly didn't want to do anything that I might fail at. Yet God kept challenging me

while things were starting to go wrong in my PR job. I'd had a brilliant manager who'd given me lots of responsibility and let me lead on huge projects, but when she left the new person wanted to run everything. He wasn't really interested in working together as a team and the other PR executive and I suffered. The whole atmosphere in the company was unsettled too, with the threat of widespread redundancies. All I kept hearing from God was "Writing is your way out", but I didn't know what that meant. I'd always had a dream about writing fiction but thought it was just that – a dream. Friends had encouraged me to take it a bit more seriously so I began thinking about a book and writing a few chapters. But now it seemed that God was saying, "Leave your job and give the writing a real go." That scared the life out of me, but every sermon I heard seemed to be on the theme of taking risks and putting yourself in a position where God absolutely had to show up or you'd be in trouble. So I prayed and prayed, chatted to wise friends for hours, and finally took the plunge. I left my job – taking voluntary redundancy, which meant I had six months' paid leave – and took a step of faith. I had my fears but I figured there is no safer bet than trusting in God to come through for you.

The first thing I realized is how intensely vulnerable it makes you, sharing your dream with other people. Some friends got it straight away and cheered me on. Other people looked at me as if I was crazy when I said I was leaving my job with nothing secure to go to. To my family, who aren't Christians, it was particularly hard to explain why I had to do this. Honestly, I felt like a complete idiot. To my own ears I sounded like a child saying, "I want to be a pop star" – it seemed like such a crazy dream to write novels. It was harder once I left work too, as I no longer had the shelter of my job to hide behind and everyone knew what I was doing.

In some ways it felt as if I'd won the lottery. I had a comfortable financial safety net, had time to spend with friends, and enjoyed creating characters and the world they lived in and watching their story unfold as I wrote. What's not to love? On the other hand, things weren't so easy. I felt insecure about my writing. Every time I sat down at my laptop I'd think: can I do this? Will the story hold together? Will I be able to finish it? Will it be any good? Will anyone ever read it? I didn't know any other fiction writers and so I felt isolated. At the same time two of my closest friends moved away, another was travelling frequently, and many more were moving on in life (getting married or starting a family). A number of people left our church at a similar time and it was a painful transition from being surrounded by amazing friends who felt like family to sometimes only knowing a handful of people on a Sunday morning. As a single person in my late twenties I was acutely aware of the lack of a partner in my life, and that in itself was a source of great pain. Finding peace was a daily struggle; it didn't come as easily as I'd experienced before – I had to search for it. It was a classic case of having stepped out of the boat and knowing that every time I took my eyes off Jesus I became uncomfortably aware that there was only water below me.

It took me six months to finish the book, but I'd finally done it: 76,000 words! I sent out the first few chapters and a synopsis to agents, wondering how and when God might do a miracle. But all that came back were rejections. Sometimes with a tiny bit of encouragement (in the form of constructive criticism), but rejections none the less. If I'd thought it was hard telling people I was writing a book, it was even harder telling them I had written a book, couldn't get it published, and so was currently unemployed. My pride took a beating every time someone asked me how it was going. One of the verses I had always clung to was Psalm 25 verse 3, which says, "Those who trust in you will never be put to shame"; I knew this was God's word but I felt ashamed. I had had no idea how much my identity and self-esteem were wrapped up in my job until it wasn't there any more.

I kept sending the book out; it kept getting rejected, and time was ticking by. The pot of money from my redundancy was starting to run dry and I was completely confused about what to do. I started to get nervous. I had presumed that God had a plan for this, and so had expected either a miraculous book deal or for him to speak to me about another job for me to go to. Neither was happening. The thought of going back to PR made me feel sick but it was all I knew and all I was trained for. My prayers became increasingly desperate, begging God to do something or say something. But everything was quiet. I had nowhere to hide. My life had no routine and no structure (again, things I hadn't appreciated about having a job until they were gone). Without work the days seemed very long and I had few distractions. I couldn't plan as I didn't know what was going to happen or when I would start working. I clung to God's word as never before, desperate to hear his voice, but I was starting to feel that he'd abandoned me. I'd thought I knew who he was and yet now I wasn't so sure. I felt as if he'd asked me to jump off a cliff and then, when I had, he'd let me smash onto the rocks below. I was reaching the end of the money (which felt like my very last bit of security) and of my emotional reserves. I didn't know if I could carry on.

For the first time, I really began to question who God was. I'd thought he was loving and kind but it was starting to seem that he might be cruel and distant; or perhaps he didn't actually exist, and then I'd really messed up my life. It was the most desperate I'd ever felt. I clung on to my faith but thought that if God was real, I must have got something wrong. I lost confidence in my ability to hear God, and in myself. What was I worth when I wasn't doing anything? I lost the hope of any good coming from the situation and I felt like an absolute mess. I didn't know how to approach God. I'd prayed about the situation in every possible way that I could and nothing had shifted, so it started to feel as if there were no words left to say. I kept going to church, and reading my Bible – taking comfort in the Psalms and the fact that the Bible itself shows us it's OK to be honest with God when we're struggling. I knew in my head that the Bible was true and God was good and he loved me, but I couldn't feel that in my heart. At the end of myself, I started going for interviews for temporary PR jobs; I just didn't know what else to do. I went through the motions but was completely conflicted about what outcome I wanted. I needed a job but knew I'd be desperately unhappy if they offered me one. I felt that I had failed. I had failed as a writer. I was failing at trusting God. I was clueless about what to do.

I'd pinned my hopes on God giving me a dramatic rescue story to tell. But the funny thing was, when he did finally speak to me one morning at church, he said, "This is the prize. Finding me here – that is the prize." I had presumed that the reward for my faith would be the outcome I was dreaming about: a publishing deal. Instead, my reward was something much greater: God wanted me to know he was with me no matter what. It's easy to see and believe he's with us when things are going smoothly, but we need to know he's with us when life is tough too. I had known that God loved me but he wanted me to know that love in a new and deeper way; a more pure way that wasn't about what he gave me but about who he is and who I am to him. I realized that if I could love God when I felt that so much had been stripped away, and if I could know he loved me there, then I would love him and know his love wherever else life took me.

One of my greatest fears was failing, and that had stopped me from doing all sorts of things. Now I knew that I had failed at something really important to me and I'd survived; it hadn't killed me! I feared too that God would overlook me, that he would forget about me, and during many of those months it had felt as if he had. But God took me to that place – and through that place – to help me face my fear and realize it wasn't true.

The fact that God had spoken to me brought a real sense of peace, even though outwardly things were still unresolved, but I was still desperate for this period to end. I wanted some certainty again and longed to know what the future might look like. I was scared that I was going to lose my house if I didn't start earning some money very soon. I started temping and it was excruciatingly painful. I was treated like an idiot – the very lowest link in the food chain. My only consolation was that it was good for my pride.

It wasn't until fifteen months after I had left my job that there was a breakthrough in my writing, but it wasn't the one I was expecting. Out of the blue my pastor asked me if I would write a book with him, and a few months later a Christian charity asked if I would do some writing for them. I was offered another opportunity to write a Christian book, and various other charities got in contact asking me to do some freelance work. I've now been writing Christian books and writing as a freelancer for charities for nine years. It was never a path I would have thought of but it's been an amazing blessing and I know I wouldn't have done it if God hadn't stripped everything else away. I wouldn't have been able to take the risks that freelancing entails (both in terms of there being regular new challenges in your work and in terms of the instability of never knowing when money is coming in). If that sounds like a nice neat ending, though, I've misled you. The desire to write fiction has never gone away, and I've since written a second full-length novel and started on a third. A number of times I've come really close to getting an agent, which is the key to finding a publisher, and then it's not happened. That's been a roller-coaster ride of getting my hopes up and then being incredibly disappointed. The journey so far has been long and painful, and although sometimes I've wanted to quit, I know God has taught me an awful lot along the way. He's dealt in large part with my desire for independence, the security I had wrongly placed in my jobs and my salary, my pride in my work, and the fact that I was a planner and a doer. I wanted people to think I was together and confident and instead I've had to let people see me as a wreck.

I had thought that if I took a step of faith, things would be straightforward as I was in God's hands, but the more I read the Bible the more I wonder where I ever got that idea from! The people who have followed God most closely have gone through crazy and faith-testing battles: Noah, having to build an ark long before the rain came down; Joshua, marching around a city wall with only faith that God could bring the wall crumbling down; David, being told he would be king but then finding his life threatened by Saul; Mary, in the shaming and life-threatening position of being pregnant outside marriage; Paul, being shipwrecked and imprisoned. And of course Jesus, the only Son of God, laying aside his majesty and communion with the Father to become a helpless baby and walk through a human life all the way to the cross. I take huge comfort and encouragement from these stories as they remind me that I shouldn't judge what God is doing by the things I can see on the surface. They show me that following God can cost us everything we have, but he's always worth it. They remind me of where my hope should be: not in the outcome that I thought might be the prize awaiting me at the end of my step of faith, but in our amazing God himself.

Chapter 5

Broken Yet Held Together by Love

Diane and I had hoped that my frame would be off in time for my fortieth birthday, but as the date drew nearer, it wasn't looking likely. As we attended yet another hospital appointment, we expected to be told that the frame needed to stay on a little longer to make sure the bones were strong enough. Instead, we were amazed when the doctor said the bones were healing well and the frame could be removed the very next day! As it was my birthday the following week we were really pleased, but once they'd checked the schedules the picture changed. I had two options: I could wait another three weeks to have the frame removed under general anaesthetic, as planned, or have it taken off that day with only gas and air. I was petrified about the pain but so desperate to get the frame off that I agreed to the gas and air. I have never felt pain like it in my life and managed to use a whole canister of gas in half an hour! The limb reconstruction nurse told me the secret to coping with pain is preparing for the process. She said the patients she worries about aren't the ones who are nervous but the ones who come in acting cocky; she knows from experience they're the ones who are likely to try to bolt when they realize quite how agonizing the procedure is. There is truth in the saying that life is 10 per cent what happens to us and 90 per cent how we react; we can't control the 10 per cent but we can control the 90. So what does it *mean* to react well? I was constantly asking myself that as I faced these challenges and disappointments. I wanted to be careful not to lapse into self-pity, but to recognize that self-awareness is a good thing and to come to terms with the fact that it's OK not to be OK. It's a good thing to be vulnerable and it's OK to ask for – and accept – help.

Do you remember – or have you seen the clips – from the 1992 Olympics where Derek Redmond was running in the 400m semi-final? As he began the sprint he tore a hamstring, leaving him in agony and unable to run. Wanting to complete the race, he hobbled along, weeping with pain and frustration. Derek's dad was in the crowd and, seeing his son in distress, he pushed past the security people and ran to his side. He wrapped his arm around Derek's shoulder and supported him as he limped the rest of the way around the track. If you look at the video closely you can see that, when his dad reached him, Derek instinctively tried to push him away before quickly realizing he wasn't going to make it on his own. He must have felt incredibly vulnerable admitting to himself, and to millions who were watching, that he wouldn't finish without his father's help. Leaning on his dad, he completed perhaps the most important race of his life, and the incident became one of the most inspiring in Olympic history, the world touched by Derek's determination and his dad's love. Derek's dad knew he needed to finish the race; he couldn't take the pain away, but he wouldn't leave him on his own. When we're in pain, what does God do? It can feel as if he's a million miles away, passively watching as we struggle on alone. Derek's dad gave us just a small glimpse of what God's Fatherly love is like. When life is painful, we have to trust what the Bible tells us about God's character: he is a loving Father, not an absent parent or an impassive dictator. Even with all my brokenness and insecurities, I need to remember that he is committed to me. Whatever is going on in our life and however it feels, he is still committed to us.

We sometimes get confused about the nature of God and our relationship with him. If we come to the Bible looking for a list of things that we need to do to get God to help us, thinking we can move God to act by our actions, we are likely to end up feeling betrayed and let down. We need to come to God's word looking for a relationship with him and seeking the loving Father behind the words on the page. Then we will find a God who loves us so much that, like Derek Redmond's father, he couldn't sit on the sidelines watching his children suffer. Instead, God came to join humanity in all our struggles and suffering, even to the point of death on the cross, and walks alongside us, carrying us and loving us. We find a Father who is present, a father we can trust and be vulnerable with.

If you'd asked me I would have said that I trusted God, but subconsciously I was wondering why God hadn't kept his side of the bargain; I was trying my hardest to do all the things I thought I should do, so where was he? I had fallen into the trap of thinking that my faith was like a legal contract. I felt as if I was honouring my side of the deal by trying to live my life for God and yet I wasn't seeing the promises of God in the Bible fulfilled (where was the promised peace and joy and life in all its fullness? Why hadn't he healed me when he had the power to do so?). What I realized was that I was treating my faith like a legal contract, in which there are obligations to fulfil on both sides – but faith is a relationship. I can seek God and love others only because I am myself loved by God, but doing those things doesn't make God love me any more. Sometimes we act as though we have to jump through a certain number of hoops to persuade a reluctant deity to love us. We don't have to fulfil certain obligations or tick a set number of boxes. God *wants* to have a relationship with us. When Jesus died on the cross he was showing us that he would give everything for us. He demonstrated once and for all that it's not about what we do – he will love us regardless.

Even in the hardest times of our life, we have to hang on to our love for him too. I was inspired by the story of Pastor Bob Sorge[19] from Canada, who, in 1992, had an ulcer in his throat and during surgery suffered a debilitating injury to his voice. Consequently, he was able only to whisper for an hour a day before the pain became too much for him. That would be devastating for anyone, but for a pastor, a speaker, and a worship leader, it went to the very heart of who he was and the things he felt God had called him to. What does a pastor do if they can't talk? What does a worship leader do if they can't sing? As well as the professional crisis, he had a theological crisis: how could Bob understand God's nature and goodness when he'd been serving and loving and

---

[19] If you'd like to hear more of Bob's story you can check out his videos and blogs at www.bobsorge.com – "I am with you" is especially worth a watch.

pouring out his life for the gospel for years and yet found himself in such a dark place with no answers? Bob says that for five years his prayer was simply "I love you. I don't understand you but I love you". He discovered that the most powerful thing he could do was to continue loving God in the midst of his confusion and pain.

Surrender

Did you ever play the game of "Mercy" as a kid? You'd twist each other's fingers and bend them back until someone cried out for mercy or surrendered. Of course, if you surrendered, you'd lost the game. In that game and in most of life, surrender is seen as a bad thing. A boxer surrenders when they can't get back up and face another round; a country shows the white flag of surrender when they know they've lost the battle. But, conversely, surrendering to God can be one of the best and most important things we can ever do. Most of us don't do it willingly. But when we're going through times when we feel that we've been pushed far beyond the limits of what we thought we could cope with, we come to the end of ourselves and finally let go. We feel broken and that brokenness allows us to admit something most of us have always known but never really liked to face: we don't have it all together. We don't have what it takes to go through life with a permanent smile on our face. We don't have the answers to every problem, and God doesn't expect us to sort things out on our own. How much time do we waste trying to resolve things using our own resources before we realize we need to go to him? Our pride tells us to try to do it alone, to keep going, and not to ask for help. I don't even think most of us recognize it as pride; our culture tends to prize independence, and we often think it's better not to risk being a burden to others. We associate pride with cocky boxers giving a press conference in which they promise to knock out their opponent or the successful business person who can't seem to help listing their accomplishments. I've always thought that pride meant loving yourself a bit too much, but I've come to see that if we can't admit our failings, insecurities, and weaknesses, we are proud. We can try to hide this behind a myriad of excuses, but it's pride nonetheless.

Conversely, there is a power in letting go. William Booth famously said, "The greatness of a man's power is the measure of his surrender." Maybe surrendering has less to do with failure and losing the game and more to do with letting go of the need for pretence. Most of us are more comfortable with people seeing our strengths than our weaknesses. Yet most of us would probably also say that the times we've felt the most loved are when we've allowed someone to see our brokenness and found they loved us regardless. Many years ago I heard a song with the lyric "broken yet held together by love". It sounded like a complete contradiction to me but now I think I understand it a bit more. Often we want to prove *why* we're lovable rather than merely accept that we are loved just as we are. In our brokenness we begin to realize it's God's unwavering love that holds us together.

Surrendering to God is about working out who is ultimately in control. It's about embracing humility – but not the clichéd image of someone who is timid and quiet and opens their mouth only to give glory to God, refusing to accept any praise. Real humility is an honest understanding of who we are – good and bad. It's about depending on God and knowing that all our strengths come from him and thus we are free to be honest about our weaknesses because we are loved regardless.

Over the years I have battled with the "why" questions: why did my friend's son get murdered? Why do I have a degenerative knee condition? Why did my dad get cancer? Why are there so many children in the world – some of whom I've known – who die of preventable diseases? People often confronted Jesus with the same type of question, for example: "Rabbi, who sinned: this man or his parents, causing him to be blind?" Jesus answered, "You're asking the wrong question. You're looking for someone to blame. There is no cause and effect here. Look instead for what God can do" (John 9:1–4, *The Message*). It's a normal human response to try to understand why suffering has entered our lives but only occasionally do people discover answers. Most of the time we're not looking for general answers about why there is suffering in the world; we're looking for something more personal. Why has it happened to us? I've found the only way to peace is to surrender these questions to God.

A few years ago I spoke at a rehab centre for recovering addicts and I loved it. In order to get into rehab an addict must be able to admit they need help, so there's an honesty and genuineness that is very refreshing to be around. The leader of the meeting, Matthew, had been clean for four years, and there were fifteen recovering addicts in the room. I sat next to Brian, who had been there only a week, and he told me his story. His parents were addicts and so he became one too at just twelve years old, going on to get involved in gangs and violence. He had been clean for three weeks when I met him, which is very early days in the process, but as he was now married, he seemed determined to stay the course. The guy leading our worship that day told me that because of his drug addiction he had lost all contact with his wife and three children. His wife had suffered so many traumas while living with him that she said she could never trust him again. I couldn't imagine how hellish it would be not to be able to see my family. Together we all stood to sing the first song, "From the Inside Out". It was so moving to be led by this former addict as he sang the line, "A thousand times I failed but your mercy remains, should I stumble again I'm caught in your grace." I had sung those words many times but as I watched this guy sing them, they took on a whole new meaning. There was so much brokenness in the room and it brought with it such a transparent honesty and desperation for God that I was envious of what they had. I wanted to be that desperate for Jesus and to call out to him the way they had. It made me think of some of the people who encountered Jesus in the Bible – the friends who lowered their mate through the roof of a house, desperate for his healing, the woman who risked public humiliation by touching the man of God though society considered her unclean because of her bleeding, the blind man who sat at the side of the road refusing to be silenced and shouting ever more loudly in his desperation. No wonder Jesus felt more at home with these people than with the religious leaders who wanted to prove how holy they were. These were the people Jesus was most attracted to, and when you've spent time with people like that you know why. There's often no pretence, just an honesty about where they're at.

My temptation is to think that I can surrender once and say "Job done", but of course true surrender has to take place day by day (and sometimes minute by minute). One of my major frustrations with myself and with this whole process of change has been that I can't honestly tell you that I've conquered all my problems. I'd love to say I used to struggle with peace but now I've learned that lesson. Tick. I used to feel angry about the suffering in the world but now I know exactly how to manage that anger. Tick. I used to feel guilty for not measuring up but now I have an assurance of grace. Tick. The fact that I *can't* tick off all these things made me question whether I should even write this book. I can't claim to be an expert, but I don't think any of us are meant to be. I think we're meant to see that we're all works in progress, slowly moving toward wholeness inch by inch, day by day. I'm not only learning but having to relearn the same lessons again and again. Amazingly, God is much more patient with the whole process than I am. I want instant fixes; he seems happy that we're heading in the right direction. I want answers and change; he wants us to keep walking hand in hand. I know I have to continually surrender to God, surrender to his plans and purposes, surrender my need for answers that I may never get, and depend on him.

The most amazing example of surrender is Jesus in Gethsemane. It always astounds me to see how Jesus was able to open his heart in complete honesty before his Father, even asking for an alternative plan. The writers of the Gospels knew it was vital to include this prayer, not feeling the need to paint a picture of a saviour who faced the cross without fear. As we read the accounts we catch a glimpse of some of the emotional and mental pressures Jesus was under. He entered the garden, which was a favourite place for him and his disciples, and went to pray as he had done many times before. But this was no ordinary night. Jesus was deeply troubled and distressed (Mark 14:33) and experts tell us the Greek verb used for troubled is "to be overcome with horror". What Jesus was facing was beyond physical torment; he knew his body faced agony but his soul faced worse. Jesus wanted the company of his closest friends, Peter, James, and John. (Another reminder to us that we're not meant to back off from those we love when we're facing trouble; we're designed to need each other.) Jesus knew he was going to die: he had predicted it time and time again, but that didn't mean he didn't fear the horror of what lay ahead. In verse 35 we read that he fell to the ground. People used to stand to pray, lifting up their hands toward heaven, but in times of severe distress they would lie flat on the ground, as King David did when his child was about to die (2 Samuel 12:16). Jesus' words in Gethsemane are well known. He cried out, "*Abba*, Father, everything is possible for you. Take this cup from me." Using the affectionate Aramaic term for father, he asked if there was any other way for their mission to be accomplished. His prayer didn't get answered with the "yes" that we presume he wanted. The cup of suffering was not taken away; there was no way around the cross. Luke records that Jesus' sweat dropped like blood to the ground, an extremely rare occurrence but one that is known to have happened to young men in World War One as they waited to go to almost certain death on the battlefield. Somehow, though, despite his extreme distress, Jesus found a way to surrender. He said, "Yet not what I will, but what you will" (Mark 14:36). He chose to trust his Father amidst the pain, anxiety, and emotional exhaustion. He chose his Father's way over his own, revealing the true nature of surrender. Far from being a moment of weakness, it shows an incredible courage and strength. I'm always amazed that Jesus managed to pray this prayer, and its words have been echoed by many Christians since. None of us can pray it lightly and most of us prefer instead to pray for God's will to match up conveniently with ours. Praying "Your will be done" means we're not in control. We're saying we're not choosing our own path; we're not going to go our own way, but instead we're going to trust in our heavenly Father come what may. For Jesus it meant suffering the agonizing pain of the cross. For us it means surrendering to things we don't always understand, following Jesus' example, resting in God's love, admitting our brokenness, and allowing him to hold us together in his love.

Chapter 6

Running on Empty

While patients are having limb reconstruction surgery it is suggested that they meet regularly with a therapist, as doctors recognize that what happens to us physically affects us emotionally. My therapist warned me that when patients have the frame removed they tend to think that they're fine and that everything will be a whole lot better, while in reality they are still in the recovery process. I nodded my head in response, understanding what she was saying but thinking that I couldn't wait to get the frame off and get back to normal life. As soon as I was free of the contraption, I threw myself head first into all the things I'd been missing out on. I picked up the kids, ran around with them, and sat playing with them on the floor. I could finally mow the grass that I'd been staring at from the sofa for so long. I waited for the euphoria to kick in: I had my life back! I could walk, I could get up off the sofa myself, I could get back to work! After a few days I noticed that I wasn't feeling that happy at all. My immediate response was to get angry with myself, thinking, "What's wrong with me? I've got the freedom I've been longing for and I should be jumping for joy." The words of the therapist came back to me: whereas I was recovering physically, I wasn't coping mentally or emotionally. Things I used to be able to do with my eyes shut were now a struggle. I led a prayer meeting at XLP, and part way through telling a story I've told many times before, I realized I had completely forgotten how the story ended. I looked out at eighty expectant faces and had no idea where I was going. Thankfully my blagging skills hadn't deserted me and I waffled on for a few minutes until my brain kicked back into gear. My memory seemed to be unreliable in other situations too. I'd find myself irritated because I didn't know all the things that were going on at XLP and then the team would say, "Remember, we spoke about this a few weeks ago?" Even with a prompt I had no recollection of the conversation.

About a week after the frame came off my parents and sister came up to celebrate my birthday, and we'd planned a meal out together in the evening. One of my wounds had started to look infected and I showed it to my mum and sister, who are both nurses. They were worried and wanted me to go to A&E, but I really didn't want to go back to hospital again and ruin our plans. We rang the ward and they told me to come straight in. They thought there might have been some gauze left in the wound, so packed it up to try to draw anything out. By the time I went back two days later they were seriously worried about an infection. It turned out that I had caught MRSA when I had gone in to A&E. When we saw the limb reconstruction nurse she was almost in tears at how unfair that was. The odds of not picking up a pin-site infection with the frame on are 1:250 and I'd been that one person; it's far less likely that you'll pick up MRSA, especially just from a visit to A&E, and yet I had contracted it. Although antibiotics cleared up the MRSA, it will unfortunately make the next operation more complicated, as there are different procedures for the hospital to follow. I might have to have the operation cancelled up to three times and will be on a far busier ward.

That hit me hard. It felt like the proverbial straw that broke the camel's back. I was so disappointed and it seemed so unfair. I had thrown myself back into work (it's not hard to get motivated in a place like XLP) but I felt as if I was running on empty and found it hard to concentrate. When I had the frame on I was embarrassed because people would comment on it all the time and there was no hiding what was going on. What I hadn't taken into account was that once the frame came off there would be no obvious external sign of the pain I was in, despite the fact I was still in recovery. It meant that I could pretend I was OK when in reality I was exhausted, frustrated, and completely at the end of myself. It felt as if this season would never end.

I would try to grab bits of rest, but it's like putting your phone on charge for five minutes when the battery is dead: you get just enough to see you through but not enough to keep you going for very long. To use another well-travelled illustration, it was like driving a car around when the petrol gauge is on red: you know you should stop and fill up but you don't have time, so you keep driving and hope for the best. As my dad constantly reminds me, this is bad for the car. We know this stuff; we know we should stop and rest, so why don't we? Why didn't I?

Mike Yaconelli said, "Rest is the ultimate humiliation, because in order to rest we must admit we are not necessary, that the world can get along without us, that God's work doesn't depend on us."[20] It can seem as if we're judged by

---

[20] Mike Yaconelli, *Messy Spirituality*, London: Hodder & Stoughton, 2001, page 113.

what we do and what we achieve, which gives us the unsettling feeling that we should always be doing something. What value will we have if we're not doing something? For many of us, exhaustion has become a status symbol. It's a standard response that when you ask someone how they are they say "Really busy" or "Things are crazy at the moment". I hear myself saying it all the time, and when someone comments on the fact that things *always* seem to be busy for me I try to justify myself, explaining exactly why this is the busiest time. I don't mean to be defensive but I find myself listing the challenges and stresses, detailing why I couldn't possibly take any time off to rest. And there's always something that tips the usual busyness of life over into the chaotic, isn't there? There's always a reason for us to put off resting. We often say we'd like another day in the week, knowing full well that if there were one we'd just fill that up too.

Global activist Lynne Twist says, "Our first waking thought of the day is 'I didn't get enough sleep.' The next one is 'I don't have enough time.'… We spend most of the hours and days of our life hearing, explaining, complaining, or worrying about what we don't have enough of.… Before we even sit up in bed, before our feet touch the floor, we're already inadequate, already behind, already losing, already lacking something. And by the time we go to bed at night, our minds are racing with a litany of what we didn't get, or didn't get done, that day."[21] If we don't address our need to keep busy and our reluctance to rest, we will constantly live with this feeling that we're behind and that life is running away from us. I felt I'd already lost enough time sitting around

---

[21] Lynne Twist, *The Soul of Money*, New York: W. W. Norton & Company, 2003, page 44.

with my frame on; I didn't want to waste any more. I wanted to be back to 100 per cent but I was still in need of rest and recuperation. There was no magic wand, no quick fix; it was going to take time. Diane kept saying to me, "You wouldn't dream of putting others under the pressure you put yourself under." So many of us do that; we set impossibly high standards for ourselves while having grace for other people. We tell them to rest when they're ill or stressed yet still try to push ourselves when we're in that position. I began to realize that it wasn't damaging just me but those around me too. I was low and irritable. I had a short fuse and would snap at people for the smallest of things. My family bore the brunt of this, which put a huge strain on my marriage, and the kids started asking Diane, "What's wrong with Daddy?" The real wake-up call for me came when Diane sat down with me one night in tears. She asked me to consider antidepressants – something she'd never asked me to do before – and it was the jolt I needed to see how this was hurting the people I loved most. I went to see my therapist and she said she could give me antidepressants but it might take up to six weeks for them to have any effect. She knew I needed to make changes straight away. I needed to start looking after myself better, not just for my sake but for the sake of those around me. I'd always struggled with the concept of compassion for oneself, as it seemed to be inward-looking or selfish, but I'd missed the point. Jesus told us to love our neighbours *as ourselves*. We can focus on the "loving our neighbours" part of that command and forget that we should love ourselves too. I realized I needed to redefine self-compassion as learning that you are a human being who is loved by God. It's about giving yourself a break. As I began to write about this on the blog, I realized how many of us do this to ourselves. One woman lost her mum to brain cancer and yet felt guilty about needing the time and space each day to take her dog for a walk, even though it was the time she felt closest to God. Another woman was thirty-seven weeks pregnant while looking after two toddlers and running a business, and the reminder that it's OK to rest brought her to tears.

Even if we know in our heads that we need to "work, rest and play", as the Mars bar adverts used to tell us, we're not always sure how to go about it. I realized I needed to be deliberate about making room for rest and relaxation in my life; they weren't just going to happen by themselves. Doing that meant I had to choose not to listen to the voices that said to me, "You can't take time off; just think about all the work you need to do. You can't play with the kids; it's not on the 'to do' list. Stop wasting time; the less you achieve today, the more you'll need to catch up on tomorrow." One thing I began doing regularly was going to the gym, as I'd not been able to exercise with the frame on. As my physical confidence grew and I got stronger, I noticed my mental health improving too. As Lewis and Webster pointed out, "Brains benefit from rest and play in equal measure, both are very important to them. And, when you get the balance right, it makes them far more efficient and effective for the work bit. Play enables your brain to lock into a less rigid mode of function than is usually allowed during periods of work."[22]

You don't often hear going to the gym, finding time to read, hanging out with close friends, or going to the cinema described as spiritual activities, but they can be vital to our

---

[22] Adrian Webster and Dr Jack Lewis, *Sort Your Brain Out: Boost Your Performance, Manage Stress and Achieve More*, Chichester: Capstone, 2014.

well-being. I find one of the times God speaks to me most is when I'm walking my dog in a local cemetery. You'd think it would be depressing, but seeing all the wildlife that flourishes in a place that's supposed to be about death reminds me that you can't keep life down; there is always growth. God is with us in the "ordinary" places as much as he is when we're at church. We can engage with him when we're hanging out with friends at the pub, playing with our kids in the park, or listening to music on our way to work. We have to find the things that relax and refresh us, and make regular space for them, committing time to them in the same way that we would to work or church duties. These aren't optional extras that we can leave out of our life without consequences; these things give us life.

Elijah: A depressed and exhausted prophet

One of my favourite Bible stories as I grew up was of Elijah the prophet. He came from an obscure place called Tishbe and lived at the time when the morally weak Ahab was king. Ahab was married to Jezebel, who was fascinated by the occult, and the people believed that Yahweh was dead. They chose to worship Baal, thought to be the god of storm and rain, elements that were very important to people who made their living from agriculture. They thought that if they gave Baal the right offerings he would look after them, and they would whip themselves and even sacrifice children in order to please him. It was in this context that Elijah told Ahab and Jezebel that there would be no more rain until he said so (1 Kings 17:1). It was a bold and hugely insulting statement;

no wonder God told Elijah to get out of there as quickly as he could. He sent him to the Kerith Ravine, where ravens fed him meat and bread, and he could drink from the brook. But with no more rain coming, the brook eventually dried up. I remember colouring in a picture at Sunday school of Elijah by this brook, in which he was depicted as lying in the glorious sunshine, enjoying what looked like some very tasty steak from heaven. The reality would have been quite different, as Kerith Ravine was hot and uncomfortable. Elijah had no human contact, no community around him, no friends to spend the day with. Only the ravens bringing food reminded him that God had not forgotten about him.

It was three years after the rain stopped that God told Elijah to go back to Ahab, and there occurred the infamous showdown between the man of God and Baal's prophets on Mount Carmel to ascertain who was the one true God (1 Kings 18). The prophets of Baal called on their god to set fire to a sacrifice they had set up. They cried out for hours until eventually Elijah began to taunt them. They prayed more loudly and even cut themselves with swords and knives in the hope that Baal would act. Yet nothing happened. So Elijah took his turn. He had twelve large jars of water poured over his sacrifice until water ran around the altar and filled the surrounding trench. Then he prayed and God's fire fell and consumed the offering. What a victory! The people fell face down, overwhelmed by what they had seen, and Elijah ordered that the prophets of Baal be put to death. Elijah knew the rain would now come after the long drought, and sure enough it did. Surely, Elijah thought, this was it; job done. God had proved himself. But Jezebel wouldn't back down. Instead, she threatened to track Elijah down and kill him. That was surely not the ending to the story Elijah was expecting. I can't imagine the overwhelming fear and disappointment he must have felt. Just because God was with him it didn't mean everything worked out smoothly, and that's something we all have to face at one point or another: things don't always work out the way we want them to. Our prayers don't always get answered with a "yes". People get ill. Relationships break down. Accidents happen. Redundancies are made. People can't always have the children they long for. Test results come back with terrifying news. I felt that I'd battled through lots of disappointments only to find that the one that broke me was getting MRSA. It was just one more in a series of confusing situations that made me wonder where God was and what he was up to. For Elijah it was all too much. He ran for his life and found himself in the desert (1 Kings 19:4). His desperation is clear from his prayer. He came to a broom bush, sat down under it, and prayed that he might die. "I have had enough, Lord," he said. "Take my life."

He didn't want to live; he couldn't see the bigger picture or see any point in carrying on. He was crushed by disappointment. I love this passage because it shows us something wonderful about how God treats us when we get to the end of ourselves. He didn't tell Elijah to cheer up, or berate him for losing faith. He didn't remind him of the great victory that had just been won and question why that wasn't enough for Elijah. He didn't make him recall previous miracles and find inspiration there. He didn't try to tell him better days were ahead if he would just keep going. Instead, he sent an angel to care for him tenderly, providing him with food so that he would have the strength for the rest of his journey. Elijah was exhausted. He didn't need a pep talk; he needed compassion. When he had regained his strength, God spoke to him in a gentle whisper: one of the most intimate encounters that we read about in the whole of the Bible. It was after that beautiful moment that God spoke again, challenging Elijah's false assumptions and telling him what he needed to do next. Elijah felt that he was the only one left. We might not be being pursued by a queen intent on our death, but in our struggles we often feel as if we're the only one going through something. The more I have opened up to others and told them about the things that are painful in my life, the more I have found how many of us are in the same boat. We all have our difficult things to deal with. Elijah might have felt alone but God reminded him that there were actually 7,000 others who hadn't bowed down to Baal (1 Kings 19:18) – though they too may have been hiding in fear from the wrath of Jezebel.

Life is full of battles and disappointments that can leave us feeling worn out, depressed, hopeless, isolated, and at the limit of our own resources. Many of us, like Elijah, have had moments when we wondered if we could even carry on any longer. These aren't the times to beat ourselves up for not having a better attitude or to criticize our ability to persevere. We have to be kind to ourselves and recognize that God doesn't demand anything from us. He loves us and wants to take care of us, as he did Elijah. He is kind to us and that's why he asks us to rest regularly. We all need to take it easy sometimes. Life takes it out of us and we need to stop seeing rest as a luxury to be squeezed in and view it as an essential part of life that fuels everything else we do.

Resting and playing well will mean we are able to work to our full potential without killing ourselves in the process. If we look after ourselves well, we will be better able to look after others. This isn't about being selfish; we're called to share in each other's sufferings and to help one another, but we can't do that if we're burned out and running on empty. Ultimately, we allow ourselves to rest when we accept that we can't earn God's love. He doesn't love us because of what we do for him and what we can achieve; he loves us because he loves us, and nothing will change that. My daughter Keziah has grown up in a multicultural school, so she can't bear to witness racism and speaks up as loudly as she can when she does. Am I proud of her for that? Absolutely. Do I love her more because of it? No; I loved her completely from the moment she was born, before she'd ever done anything, and nothing can change that. Love isn't based on performance but on relationship. Sometimes the only way we can know that for sure is when we let go of our need to achieve every minute of every day.

Chapter 7

Second-hand Smoke: Diane's Story

Diane and I began dating when I was fifteen, having met at school, and we got married six years later. We've now been married for eighteen years so she knows me better than anyone and has seen both the best and the worst of me. Diane is a more positive person than I am by nature so at times she's had to drag me along and try to keep my spirits up, but the things that I have been through have of course taken their toll on her too. Often the person who is in physical pain gets all the attention but the people caring for them have to face many extra burdens. I asked Diane to tell her side of the story as I know there's a suffering in seeing those you love suffer and in having to look after them. Through everything that's happened Diane has been amazing, and I would have gone insane without her.

> I can clearly remember the moment when I found out Patrick had to have the operations on his knees. It was January 2008 and I was walking around the chiller section in Sainsbury's on my own, newly pregnant with Abigail, our third child. As Patrick told me the shocking news over

the phone, I was crying so much I couldn't see what I was looking at, let alone remember what I was supposed to buy.

When I first met Patrick, back in 1989, he was extremely passionate about football. I came from a family who knew nothing about the game but when we started going out, I regularly went to watch him play and even learned the offside rule. One Saturday when we'd been married a few years he came home limping, saying he'd been kicked in the knee during a game. Little did we know that this would be the start of years of trouble. The pain never fully went away. Over the years it slowly got worse until he was told he would never play again. It's so hard seeing someone you love denied one of their greatest pleasures. I had previously tried to be positive and reassure him that things would eventually get better but now I knew that wasn't true. When we knew he had to have surgery, I wanted to get on with it right away. I like to plan and hate to be in limbo, so thought it would be best just to get it over with. Patrick, on the other hand, wanted to delay the procedure as long as possible so that he could in turn delay the knee replacements that would inevitably come afterwards, so I had to go along with his timing and deal with the operation hovering over our heads like a storm waiting to break.

I was so proud of all the ways that Patrick tried to delay the operations by keeping himself fit and healthy, but meanwhile I wasn't doing very well. I loved our three children and desperately wanted a fourth. I was one of five and loved the noise and chaos of a large family; it seemed normal to me and I had always assumed this was the life I would have as a parent myself. Even before Abigail was a year old I was ready to start thinking about child number four, but Patrick wasn't sure. I prayed that God would either take the desire from me or change Patrick's heart, and clearly felt God say, "Trust me." Shortly after this, I fell pregnant. This was my miraculous gift from God and I was so grateful. Like any woman who is longing for a child, from the moment I found out I was expecting I began making plans and imagining the future, but at thirteen weeks I started bleeding. This had happened while I was carrying Abigail and everything had been completely fine, so I wasn't worried. So when the sonographer said they were having difficulty finding the baby's heartbeat during the scan, I couldn't believe what I was hearing. I was told it looked as if the baby had stopped growing at nine weeks. I was trying to get my head around this shocking news when they said they needed to book me in for an operation to remove the "products of conception". That was my baby they were talking about; that was my future, my hope, my gift from God. I was numb. We named the child Joel and for a while afterwards he was still very much part of our family. As Patrick has told you, we were fortunate enough to get pregnant again a little while later, and despite a difficult birth, we were so happy to welcome Caleb into our family. We were complete.

During this time we built an extension on our house to make some extra space. We spent thirteen weeks over the summer moving from place to place while a good part of the house was gutted. It was chaotic but Patrick kept going. It was so hard to see him deteriorating in front of my eyes, though. We couldn't go for long walks any more, or climb mountains as we used to. Even kicking a ball around in the park was painful. Patrick couldn't pick up or hold Caleb much and bending down to pick things up was impossible. Once we'd seen the consultant to book the operation we knew there were at least three hard years ahead of us, and it was strange trying to prepare for that. There were loads of practicalities to take care of but I was particularly scared about my relationship changing from that of wife to carer. I wasn't sure how to get ready. I'm useless with blood and the sight of the frame made me feel ill. I wasn't sure I'd have enough patience either. My biggest fear was that I would get frustrated, impatient, and angry with Patrick, and I was desperate to find a way not to. I tried to do some research about ways to prepare for caring for a spouse but all I managed to find were a few forums for people who care for spouses or family members suffering from dementia or Alzheimer's. They didn't make for easy reading and most were saying they were experiencing all I feared I would.

The summer before the operation we tried to cram in all the good things we could as a family, knowing there were difficult times ahead. We also had to apply for secondary schools for our eldest daughter, and I felt completely alone. Patrick was busy at work and I felt the full weight of responsibility for finding the right school for Keziah, knowing it could affect our other children too. I was juggling working hard for a local charity, trying to visit schools, and trying to arrange extra help with the kids so I would be able to visit Patrick in hospital. I wasn't able to take any leave as we needed to save the holiday for after Patrick's operation. It all got too much. I felt as if I would fall over if even a tiny feather touched me. I had always been the strong one but at this point, when my strength and ability to cope were most needed, it seemed that they had deserted me. I needed help and the doctor gave me some medication for anxiety to help me keep going.

When Faith Gets Shaken

When the day of the operation finally came, Patrick seemed oddly calm but I was so worried about him. Seeing him being wheeled into the room on a bed with the huge frame on was one of the worst things I have ever seen in my life. He looked so broken. The next nine days were a blur of being at Patrick's bedside while the doctors tried to find the right medication and we attempted to deal with his anxiety. I was shown how to change his dressings, a painstaking job that would become my responsibility once we got home. He had loads of different contraptions to use to make sure his muscles didn't stop working, despite not being used. Any time he wanted to move it was a big deal. He had so many pillows to make him comfortable, yet he couldn't get comfortable. He was told to rest, yet told to move. He was told to keep his leg up, but not too high. He was told to take painkillers, but not get reliant on them. It was all very confusing. When he was allowed home, we were pleased but petrified. He was in agony, and adjusting to being outside hospital was frightening. My strong husband was in pieces. How the hell were we going to get through this? It was that evening that I cried out to God and he gave me the picture of a tunnel, showing me he was with us and would help us make it through by focusing on the now, rather than the length of the journey ahead. At some points it was necessary to focus on just one hour or even one minute, let alone a whole day. We quickly realized we needed to set up the house differently and had all sorts of new challenges to face, such as finding a chair that Patrick could get in and out of independently, and figuring out a way for him to shower that involved lots of different devices. Night-times were the hardest. I had to strap him into his contraptions, put the right pillows in the right places, and lay the covers just so. I would just be falling asleep when he needed to go to the toilet, and of course he couldn't get there alone. I would have to unstrap and remove everything, get him up onto his crutches, and help him navigate his way to the bathroom. This happened several times through the night. Changing his dressings and doing his alterations (adjusting the pin struts over a period of time) was stressful and complicated. But slowly we got used to the frame being part of our lives and developed a new routine.

Living with someone who was temporarily disabled was an eye-opener. It's a very lonely experience. I couldn't go out, as I couldn't leave Patrick alone with the children but I couldn't get a babysitter as Patrick would feel strange being there too. Though we worked out how to get Patrick into the car, it wasn't comfortable, so we couldn't go very far. There were endless hospital trips and visits and I tried to go with him, even though most of the appointments lasted four hours plus. I have a friend whose husband is chronically ill and it was a comfort to have someone who understood the pressures and frustrations of these times. You lived from one piece of news to the next, not knowing how long situations would last for, or what you were looking for. You were at the mercy of X-rays and blood test results. Every time you hoped for something positive, the story would change or what you were looking for would change. Your whole world is centred on (in our case) the frame, and when it is going to come off. Patrick did everything that was asked of him. I would often walk into a room and he was again in a strange position doing one of his exercises.

As Patrick's fortieth birthday approached, I wanted to organize something that he would remember and which would be a positive experience during this hard time. Of course our options were limited by the frame still being there, so I organized a concert at our local pub. Then everything was up in the air again when we were told the frame could come off earlier than expected. Suddenly we were scared once more. Although all we wanted was to get the frame off, we had got used to it and felt strangely safe with it. The fact that he got an infection on the day of his birthday surprise was just another reminder that we couldn't plan anything as the operation was still taking charge of our lives. I wondered if I'd made a terrible mistake in planning a surprise gathering, but didn't want to cancel. So much effort had gone into it and friends and family were coming from far and wide to celebrate with Patrick. Thankfully, having dosed himself up, Patrick was able to be there despite feeling rough, and we were able to celebrate with the friends and family who had been so good to us.

It's now six months later and life is, relatively, back to normal. But I think our definition of "normal" may have changed. I am definitely not the same person I was before. I'm not as strong as I used to be, or as "together". I'm definitely not as independent as I was and I find it harder to make decisions. I used to be an extrovert; now I find it harder to be around people. I came off my medication very slowly but I still get days of intense stress and anxiety. I never used to experience this; is this the fallout after the crisis? I don't know. What I do know is this: we did it. We got through it. Patrick is amazing and my children are champions. God is my absolute rock. Without him, I would crumble. We have to go through the whole thing again but

SECOND-HAND SMOKE: DIANE'S STORY

I know now that we will get through it. My coping strategy still is to live in the moment, one day at a time, being content with where I am, with what I have, and with who I am. I'm having to relearn how to build myself up, as two people running on empty is not a good combination. One of the ways I have been doing this is by going swimming early in the morning. That hour is precious – no one can come and find me, call me, ask me a question, get me to do something, or ask me for a drink or to find their shoes.

It was Patrick who had to deal with the physical pain and go through the operations but I still felt the impact. It was a bit like inhaling second-hand smoke. You may never pick up a cigarette yourself but being around a chain-smoker means your lungs will inhale the tar too. Second-hand smoke may be dangerous but I was interested to read that "primates that groom each other after a stressful event experience a reduction in blood pressure". Experts go as far as to say that "grooming others has a greater impact than getting groomed".[23] Although going through tough times is hard, going through them together makes you stronger. It also makes you appreciate the good times in life much more. There is nowhere else I would rather be than right by Patrick's side.

---

[23] http://www.webmd.com/balance/features/why-youre-not-happy

Chapter 8

Guilt

"I'm letting everyone down... I should be able to handle this... I ought to be better now... this is all my fault." These were the types of thought running around my head as I daily did battle with overwhelming guilt. I could see the toll everything was taking on Diane and I couldn't help but feel responsible. I knew I hadn't intentionally done anything to lead us into this situation, but I still struggled to let go of the guilt.

Of course, there are two types of guilt: true (legitimate) guilt and false (unhealthy) guilt. True guilt is something we need to listen to. It's the nagging feeling when we know we've done or said something we shouldn't have and we need to rectify it, or when we've left something undone that should have been done. It pushes us to be better, to learn from our mistakes, to make amends, and to move forward positively. False guilt is something else altogether. It's when we worry we may have upset someone without any real proof that we actually have. It's when we text someone, don't get an instant reply, and begin to think through all the things we could have done wrong that might have upset them. We can get into patterns of thinking like this, assuming we have done something wrong, worrying we're letting people down, and feeling guilty about things that are quite possibly a figment of our imagination. We can also experience false guilt over things that are outside our control. Someone who has been abused or cheated on will often feel guilty despite the fact they did nothing wrong. When somebody we love turns out to be someone different from who we thought they were, we blame ourselves for being stupid and not seeing what was happening.

In Will van der Hart and Dr Rob Waller's recently published work *The Guilt Book*, they explore this topic in more depth and give some very helpful and practical advice on dealing with true guilt and false guilt. Will is a pastor and Rob a psychiatrist, so they have spent a lot of time listening to people who are struggling in this area. They say the words that come up time and time again are "should, must, ought, always, and never":

> *I should always be ready for anything that might happen.*
> *I must be a good friend whenever anyone calls.*
> *I ought to have seen that coming.*
> *I always make sure nothing bad will happen.*
> *I will never allow chance to play its part.*
> *I will always be in control so no one can hurt me.*
> *I will never allow anyone to hurt me again.*[24]

If we find ourselves using these words frequently, we may well be allowing false guilt to be in control of our lives, setting ourselves impossible standards, and making vows we can't and shouldn't keep. I know that, for me, guilt crept into

---

[24] Will van der Hart and Rob Waller, *The Guilt Book*, Nottingham: IVP, 2014, page 32.

my spiritual life too. I felt guilty that I felt so bleak and my relationship with God didn't seem as good as I wanted it to be. This was compounded by all the people who had said this enforced rest would be my chance to spend hours with God. I had hoped that, while I wasn't able to run around and do things, I would have more space to hear God's voice. Some suggested this might be God's hidden purpose in it all: that he was giving me time to spend with him. Yet my prayers seemed to bounce off the ceiling. I couldn't find the energy to get stuck in to all the great theology books sitting in a big pile taunting me. I couldn't get away from the feeling that I *should* be having intimate communion with God, when it was very obvious that I wasn't.

I realized that often when I tried to pray or read my Bible my motivation was guilt rather than relationship. We can so easily use the amount of time we spend praying and reading the Bible as a measure of the state of our relationship with God. Got that magic half-hour in this morning? Great! You're set up for the day and you are officially a committed Christian. Missed it? The voice in our head says that makes us a failure and questions our commitment to God. I heard of a home group who were discussing how long they prayed each day. The first person said they tried to have at least an hour, the second person said something similar, and so it continued until they got to a mum who had recently had a baby. She just burst into tears, overwhelmed with guilt that she didn't manage to pray that much at all. Sometimes we make these disciplines into yardsticks and judge ourselves and each other by them rather than knowing that our relationship with God is about so much more than ticking a box on Bible reading or prayer. I remember when I first started speaking at festivals I met a well-known speaker for the first time, and this person asked me, "How many times have you read the Bible all the way through from beginning to end?" I choked on my coffee and tried to make up a quick excuse for why I hadn't managed it yet. I went into my first meeting feeling like a complete idiot who had no right to be there, rather than a normal guy who loves God's word but hasn't made it through all of Leviticus. Don't get me wrong: praying and reading the Bible are both crucial elements of being in a relationship with God, but I wish we could have the right motivations for doing them and let go of the guilt we so often attach to them. Usually we beat ourselves up for not doing "enough", but what *is* "enough"? We're creating a self-defeating goal that can leave us trapped in guilt rather than coming to God out of love and relationship. Even in hospital when I was still drowsy from painkillers, I was aware of this voice telling me I should be using the time to pray. I was struggling to hold a thought in my head for a few seconds but I still felt guilty. A hospital chaplain came to see me and I nervously shared how I was feeling, awaiting her verdict and the condemnation I felt I deserved. Instead, she said, "My advice to you is *not* to pray." I thought I'd misheard her through my post-surgery fog. It seemed like a strange thing for a godly woman in a dog collar to be telling me.

"What do you mean?" I said cautiously, waiting for the catch. "You've just gone through major surgery; the last thing you need is to be lying there feeling guilty because you're not praying. God understands. You have so many people praying on your behalf; let them carry you in prayer for a while." It was the opposite of the advice I thought I would get, yet it was incredibly liberating. I started to give myself a break and tried to give my mind a rest from all the striving to do what I thought was right.

Pleasing everyone

We all have an inner perfectionist – for some of us it rears its head every now and then because we want to please people; for others it is like an addiction that controls and consumes us. The perfectionist in us is great at making us feel guilty. It sets us up with unrealistic expectations, wanting everything we do to be flawless, and then we beat ourselves up when we don't hit the mark. The perfectionist's favourite phrases are the guilt mantras of "I should… I must… I ought to… I have to…". Nothing is ever enough. There is always something more to do or another way to improve. A perfectionist can struggle to celebrate their achievements or to revel in the 90 per cent of their day in which they did well; they focus instead on the 10 per cent that didn't go as planned and feel like a failure because of it. Guilt and perfectionism undermine our self-confidence and leave us feeling totally inadequate. I know I give the perfectionist in me more airtime than I should, and while we can still see it as the perfect answer to the interview question "What's your greatest flaw?", it *is* a flaw, and one that needs to be dealt with.

When we feel we have to be perfect we procrastinate more before making a big decision, as we fear making the wrong decision. We find it hard to take even constructive criticism because we can't accept that the things we do are less than perfect. No wonder perfectionism can lead to depression and severe anxiety. Trying to be perfect is not the same as trying to do your best. That, of course, is a great goal we should all work toward. As Will van der Hart and Dr Waller point out, "Perfectionism is a class A drug to those who suffer with false guilt. What is more, few places (including churches and businesses) dissuade their members from use."[25]

Church should be the place where perfectionism is discouraged, as it's the opposite of grace. God's grace is his unmerited favour and love, given freely to us by our loving Father who sees who we are truly are and loves us anyway. Perfectionism says we have to earn our value and are not worthy of love unless we get everything right all of the time. It's hard to experience God's grace when we're clinging on to our need to get things right. Dallas Willard helpfully points out, "Grace is not opposed to effort, it is opposed to earning. Earning is an attitude; effort is an action."[26]

For me, trying to embrace grace meant learning not to suppress the thoughts and feelings that were going through my head. Pretending I wasn't feeling guilty wasn't going to help me but I also learned to see which other feelings were piggybacking on my guilt, such as shame and frustration. I'm learning to be honest with myself and others. I'm learning that when I fail, it doesn't help if I beat myself up endlessly. I need to accept God's forgiveness and forgive myself. I had to stop saying, "I should, I must, I have to…" and instead set myself realistic goals that I might achieve and learn to cope with it if I don't achieve them.

---

[25] *The Guilt Book*, page 107.
[26] http://www.goodreads.com/quotes/49184-grace-is-not-opposed-to-effort-it-is-opposed-to

We all hear voices

The essential thing to remember is that God doesn't want us to feel guilty. When we have done something wrong, he convicts us so that we can turn away from the thing we've done and receive his forgiveness. Satan, on the other hand, loves to make us feel guilty and is delighted if we wallow in our guilt and shame for as long as possible. While we continue to hang on to guilt we're listening to the enemy's whispers of condemnation, which leave us feeling unworthy, unlovable, and like complete failures instead of embracing the grace of God's forgiveness.

Do you remember the film *A Beautiful Mind*, starring Russell Crowe? It's a biographical film about the life of John Nash, a mathematical genius who also suffered from schizophrenia. Nash heard voices of government officials telling him he needed to break Soviet codes, causing him to have a major breakdown in which he believed he was in the midst of a huge and terrifying conspiracy. Over time Nash had to learn to tell the difference between real human voices and the ones he was imagining. He managed to do it so successfully that he went on to win a Nobel Memorial Prize for his work. During the scene in the film in which someone comes to talk to Nash about the prize for the first time, he is wary. He has learned to be cautious about voices that play to his desire to be important and significant. He stops a passing student and asks, "Do you see a man standing there? Is he in your line of vision? Is he for real?" Only when the student says yes does Nash turn back to the man and agree to listen. Nash had to find ways of protecting himself from listening to the wrong voices, and isn't that true of all of us?[27] Don't we sometimes need to take something to a friend and ask them if the voice can be trusted? Are the voices we hear constantly positive or constantly negative? We all sometimes need someone who can help us discern when God is challenging us and when we are feeling needlessly guilty.

I know that a powerful voice in my life over many years has been the voice of comparison, which tells me that everyone else is more capable, efficient, and intelligent than I am. If I'm speaking at a festival, I can't help but check out the programme when I arrive to see who is speaking at the same time as me. The voice in my head says, "They are really funny; they have some amazing stories of how God has worked in Africa; they are incredibly intelligent and wise." I'll always find a reason to find myself wanting, and after a few minutes of reading about the other speakers I will have managed to convince myself that there is no point in my being there at all, as I have nothing to contribute. My "impostor's syndrome" kicks in (that's the voice that tells me everything I have ever achieved is just a fluke and makes me worry that one day I'll be found out as being useless). Just a few minutes of comparison and I'm hunting out my satnav, desperate to go home. The crazy thing is, it's not even about being "good enough" anyway; it's about being willing to make yourself vulnerable in order for God to work through you. After I have spoken I'll often hear the voice of self-criticism, beating myself up for things I should have done differently.

I constantly hear negative voices about my parenting too. I confess I sometimes get a moment's pleasure when I see

---

[27] This illustration is adapted from John Ortberg, *God Is Closer Than You Think*, Grand Rapids, MI: Zondervan, 2005.

someone else's kid having a tantrum in a public place, as it reminds me I'm not the only one it happens to. I pressurize myself that I *must* be the perfect parent and that if my kids are kicking off, it must always be my fault. These voices are loud, and it can be difficult to tell them to shut up because it's often easier to believe the bad stuff about ourselves than the good. We have to learn to tune in to another voice, though: one that isn't destructive, one that doesn't point out everything we have done wrong or have been too exhausted to finish; a voice that says I AM ENOUGH.

Many psychologists encourage people to do that by sitting in one chair to talk about a memory or situation that they feel guilty about. For me, that was thoughts like, "I can't achieve anything. I should be back to 100 per cent at work by now. People around me are bearing the brunt of this and getting exhausted." The psychologist encourages you to note the accompanying feelings that the thoughts bring, such as guilt, anxiety, frustration, and feeling useless. You then switch chairs and respond to the things you've just said, putting yourself in the position of a friend or Jesus, and imagining what they might say in response to you. Those words are likely to be much kinder: "You are doing so well; no one is expecting you to be better already; your friends and family love you and want to take care of you." I used to think this type of activity was a waste of time and wouldn't help in any way, but it has enabled me to understand and practise the discipline of questioning the negative voice and being open to hearing an alternative one. You could even try recording your kinder voice and playing it back to yourself when you start to hear the negative voice. Jesus' voice is one of grace and love; his is the voice of one who laid down his life for us, who longs for us to be free and to know we are a son or daughter who is truly loved. We need to learn to discern his voice over all the others (both in our own head and in the world around us), as his is the opinion that matters. We need to make space to hear that still, small voice.

Even in the Bible we see that people didn't always recognize God's voice. In 1 Samuel 3 we read that the Lord called Samuel three times, but Samuel kept thinking it was Eli's voice until Eli instructed him to say, "Speak, Lord, for your servant is listening" (verse 9). God's voice was so normal that Samuel thought it was human. Is there a danger that we might think we'll hear God's voice only in church meetings or when we're praying, rather than listening for him in any ordinary moment, waking or sleeping? Jesus said that he was the good shepherd and that his sheep would recognize his voice (John 10:11–18), but maybe, like Samuel, we have to learn to hear and discern God's words against the background noise of all the voices in the world around us. This is the voice I long to hear more clearly in my life. It's the voice of love that refuses to heap more guilt on those who are already so aware of their sin and weakness. All those who approached Jesus in the humility of knowing their own sin left his presence feeling valued and full of hope for their future. How often do we subconsciously attribute the "must try harder" voice to God rather than listen to hear his words of love, loyalty, and kindness? After Jesus' arrest we see how Peter messed up and denied that he even knew the messiah, but after Jesus rose again Peter accepted the grace that Jesus offered him. Judas, on the other hand, having also betrayed his friend, never gave himself the chance to see if grace would be offered to him. We need to come to God with our hands open, ready to receive as Peter did, not with our fists closed, fearful, like Judas, of what we will hear. As we learn to walk in his grace, dependent on him, we can begin to let go of our need to perform and our pointless guilt, instead allowing his gentle Father's voice to convict us where necessary and clothe us with grace to carry on. We can work hard to earn other people's praise and affirmation but will it ever be enough? Or we can trust in our relationship with God and accept that he is for us and with us whether we've hit our self-imposed spiritual targets or not, learning to let go of our guilt and to depend on his grace.

Hannah's Story

Hannah has been working with us at XLP for a number of years and she is now our mentoring manager in Lewisham. She works with young people on the margins of society and finds them a mentor who is willing to spend two hours a week with them over twelve months. Hannah is kind and generous and has always been known for laughing a lot. In 2012 I had just arrived home from the Soul Survivor summer conferences and crawled into bed at 1 a.m., exhausted. When all the phones in the house started ringing just a few hours later, at 6 a.m., I knew that something was seriously wrong. It was Simon, XLP's Chief Operating Officer, and he told me that Hannah's sixteen-year-old son, Nathaniel, had been stabbed through the heart and killed in the early hours of the morning. I felt physically sick. My mind went numb trying to process such horrendous information. I was lost for words. I couldn't believe something so terrible could happen to such an amazing woman. I have no idea how Hannah has carried on and how she has managed to continue working and serving others so selflessly. Her faith and her ability to persevere have inspired me. This is her story about Nathaniel.

> Nathaniel was the youngest of my three children. When I found out I was pregnant with him I was shocked; we

hadn't planned on having any more kids and it was a complete surprise. I sailed through the pregnancy but the birth was horrendous and I ended up in hospital for two weeks. With my first two children, Jermaine and Helina, I had gone back to work fairly soon, but with Nathaniel I was able to stay at home with him so I have many precious memories of those early days. He was very vocal and very clingy as a baby, and everywhere I went he was attached to my hip. Jermaine and Helina adored him. Helina, who was ten years old when he was born, treated him as if he was her baby and we used to joke that there were three parents in the house. As a toddler, he was very energetic and always on the move. Jermaine would dare him to do things and he had no sense of fear so he'd always give it a shot. He even tried climbing a wall after watching Spider-Man!

When he started school, he quickly got into football and would play every day. By the time he was seven, his teacher had spotted that he had talent and invited him to join a local team. He loved it and made some good friends too. He would play outside our home in a panna cage and would take on anyone, even if they were older than him. The older kids said they thought he'd make it as a pro footballer as he was so quick and agile, plus he could score with both feet. To Nathaniel, football was life. Even at secondary school he would get up an hour early just so he could squeeze in some more practice before lessons started. He played at school and in a local league and got scouted for Southend. For a while we would travel down from London each evening for him to train and then at weekends for games, which were sometimes on a Saturday and a Sunday, but he never got bored by it. The travelling did get too much, though, so when he was offered a trial at Charlton, he took that instead. He was doing well academically but enjoyed being the class clown and was always making people laugh. The way he and his brother would tease each other would have us all in hysterics; they were like Laurel and Hardy. Nathaniel's outlook was to have fun and to make the most of every opportunity.

When he was fourteen, Nathaniel went to Holland for a football tournament with the boys from the years above him, as the teacher said he was good enough to make their team. He came back on fire and so proud that they had come second in the league and he had medals and trophies to prove it. Not long afterwards, though, he got injured and couldn't play. It coincided with a growth spurt and he had terrible pain in his knees, so the physio said he had to rest or he would aggravate the injury. He took it really hard. He started hanging out with some local boys who I knew had been involved in drug dealing, and one night when he came home I could tell he'd been smoking. I knew he'd lost his confidence; he was feeling really low and wasn't sure what to do with himself without football in his life. It felt as if he was going off the rails and we wanted to help him find his way again. His sister suggested he think about going into sports physiotherapy and he was keen, but when he stopped hanging around with that group of boys to try to get back on track, they began making threats against him and we were seriously worried for his safety. We decided the best thing to do was to leave the area as a family and for Nathaniel to move schools. As he settled in, he slowly started to seem like the old Nathaniel again.

We planned a family trip to Grenada as my sister was getting married there, and Nathaniel loved it. He had so much fun hanging out with his cousins and connecting with his wider family. Everything is so laid back there and so safe that you don't even need to lock your front door – quite the opposite of London! Nathaniel talked about going back in the future, maybe even to live there, as he enjoyed it so much. In many ways it was a significant time for him. Although he had grown up in church and believed in God, he had been backsliding for a while. In Grenada he started asking lots of questions about life and faith; he was clearly searching for meaning and wondering where his life was going. Nathaniel found it hard that his own dad wasn't in his life; we divorced when Nathaniel was three and his dad wasn't around for him, which of course was painful. I encouraged him to talk to God about those feelings. He was compassionate to others too. One of his friends was going through a bad time and he really wanted to support him; he felt really deeply that life can be cruel. After we talked, he said he wanted to make some changes to his life and be a good influence on his friends. He was back on track as regards thinking about his future, and said he wanted to try to be a sports physio and see if he could play football too. He took his GCSEs and got seven, so I was really proud of him, especially as we'd moved again so there was yet another transition for him. We arranged a placement for him through a friend who worked at the Professional Footballers' Association and he was looking forward to getting stuck in to that. He had an interview lined up for college and was already excited, planning on wearing a new suit even though they didn't expect him to be that smart.

On 28 July 2012 we celebrated Nathaniel's sixteenth birthday with lots of his friends. We had a meal together and then prayed for him; he was the happiest I'd seen him in a long time. Nathaniel spent the next couple of nights staying with his best friend, Juan. I spoke to him on the phone and we arranged to meet the following day so I could bring him home. As I rang off I said, "Keep safe."

"Yeah, Mum," he replied. In the early hours of the next morning the phone rang and I knew something was wrong. Helina sounded frantic as she said that Nathaniel had been hurt; he was in Downham and we needed to get there ASAP. Minutes later Jermaine called and said he was on his way and would call back when he knew more. Desperate to get there as quickly as we could, I woke my husband and we jumped into the car. I picked up the first thing I could find to wear and it happened to be my XLP T-shirt that says, "Hope is the refusal to accept a situation as it is". As we drove, everything seemed to slow down around me; it was agony not knowing what was going on. I frantically called Helina and Jermaine but they didn't answer. Every minute felt like an hour; I needed to get to Nathaniel's side. I kept saying to God, "Why Nathaniel? Why did he have to get hurt?" As we got to where Nathaniel's friend lived we saw that the police had cordoned off the road to stop people from going any further. I phoned my daughter and she immediately rushed over. The police asked who I was and they let me through.

Helina said, "Nathaniel didn't make it."

I couldn't take in what she was saying; I couldn't have heard her right, so I asked, "What do you mean?"

"He's been stabbed and he's dead," she replied. My immediate thought was no! It can't be Nathaniel; there has to have been a mistake.

"I need to see him. Where is he?" I cried.

"You can't, Mum. The police have taped up the house; you can't go in." I ran toward it anyway and tried to push past the police standing there. They tried to hold me back but I kept trying saying, "If he's dead, I need to see him." Suddenly Jermaine appeared and took hold of me, leading me away and telling me the same thing I'd just heard, trying to make me take in something that my brain had no ability to comprehend. Nathaniel was dead. My Nathaniel. Gone.

Slowly I began to piece together what had happened. Nathaniel was staying with Juan and they'd gone over to Juan's girlfriend's house as her parents were away for the weekend. She had invited a few friends over, including two young lads Nathaniel didn't know. Nathaniel was his usual jokey self, having fun and saying hi to everyone, and the two boys asked who he was. Nathaniel blanked them and when they asked again, he said, "It's nothing to do with you." Nathaniel messaged one of his cousins to say he didn't like the way the boys were looking at him and he didn't feel safe. He decided to leave, saying in a text, "Death is round the corner; he's coming like a flood." There was a fight but the boys said they didn't want any trouble, so Nathaniel sat down to wait for the taxi he'd called. But one of the boys couldn't leave it. As I understood it at the time, he walked over to Nathaniel and said, "I don't like the way you're carrying on." Nathaniel ignored him and the guy felt he was being disrespected, so he stabbed him. One of the girls there saw Nathaniel get up but then fall over; he managed to tell her he'd been stabbed and the guy who did it ran out. That's why they wouldn't let me see my son: the house was a crime scene and his body was evidence. That was one of the worst things about it, that I couldn't touch my precious boy to say goodbye. I couldn't hold his hand or hug him one last time. We were only allowed to see him from behind a glass screen the following day. The police had to do an autopsy, which of course is hugely invasive, and meant his body couldn't be released for burial straight away.

I have been a Christian for most of my life but suddenly I felt completely disconnected from God. During those early days it was unbearable even to try to talk to God. All I had were "why" questions going around and around in my head. I had no words to pray; all I could do was cry. I felt lost and walked around in a daze for a long, long time. I would find myself somewhere with no recollection of how I had got there. I didn't want to live without my son; it was just too painful. It wasn't that I wanted to kill myself; I just didn't want to be here any more. Some days I would go through the motions. Other times I would spend the whole day in bed crying. I didn't want to see anyone or talk to anyone; I knew there was no one who could do anything to ease the pain.

It was only a few days after Nathaniel's death that I was sitting in my church for the service of peace that we'd been planning at XLP for the previous few months. The idea was to bring groups together from neighbouring – and often warring – postcodes to pray together. So many young people were losing their lives because of gun and knife crime that we wanted to gather affected communities to pray together. I never imagined I'd be sitting in that service as a mother who had lost her own child to knife crime. As we listened to stories of young people who had been stabbed or shot but had survived, I was desperately crying out to God, asking him why my son hadn't survived too. Why didn't you do it for me, Lord? Why didn't you save my boy? Why take him when he was in the prime of his life? Why take him when he'd just turned a corner and started feeling positive about his future? Why? Why? Why?

I went to church over the following weeks and months but I found worship too hard and would have to walk out, finding somewhere quiet I could sob. Most of my friends were brilliant but occasionally someone would say something like "It will get better", and I'd want to slap them. How the hell could life get better with Nathaniel gone? Others would try the old clichés, telling me God had a plan, or seemingly trying to get me to push past my grief, but that didn't help me either. Even hearing people say "God is good" is hard when you're in so much pain. Some people avoided me, presumably because they didn't know what to say. I don't think there are any words that help in a situation like that. But one Sunday a lady came up and just hugged me without saying anything, and that was exactly what I needed. As she held me I felt as if God was saying, "I've got you. It's going to be alright." It was the first time I'd felt peace since Nathaniel died.

Over time my mood switched from numb to angry. I never doubted God was in control and I knew I loved him, but at the same time I was so angry with him. Nothing made sense. It's human nature to ask "Why?", but if you've ever been through something as painful as this you'll know that you can drive yourself insane trying to find answers to why it happened. My husband bore the brunt of my anger and I lashed out at him. He felt that he could never say the right thing, and of course he had his own grief to deal with too.

The nightmare continued when we had to face the boys who took Nathaniel's life in court. They were bold enough to look us in the eyes, showing no remorse about what had happened. Because I've worked with young people for years, I understand the culture they're growing up in and the way they are with each other. I wasn't angry with them – although I'm not sure that I've forgiven them yet – but I do understand what life is like for them. I can see they are troubled boys who have many problems in their lives, but I still knew that my son deserved justice over what had happened. The boys were tried for murder but the jury decided they had acted in self-defence and so they walked free. I was devastated. The boys laughed as they left court but all I was left with were more questions. Where was the justice for Nathaniel?

Some days I feel that I trust God; other days I don't know what to do with myself and feel that I just want to bang my head against a wall. I find it hard to sleep with so many unanswered questions floating around my head so sometimes I just get up and sit for a while. It's human to want answers to why something like this happens, but after a while I realized that Jesus never answered the "why" questions. There could never be an answer that would be good enough to explain why I lost my son in such a way. At some point you have to find a way to live without knowing, otherwise the search for answers will drive you mad.

In some ways I can see God at work, though. When it first happened, there was so much anger from Nathaniel's friends that I feared there would be reprisals and more violence. (It's common for revenge attacks and killings to take place in situations like this.) But even after the verdict they managed to control themselves, and I'm really grateful for that. Killing someone else wouldn't bring Nathaniel back; it would only wreck more people's lives. Working at XLP has been a huge blessing while I've been grieving and I really sense God in that. The team are great and it's an environment where you can be real about what's going on. Our offices are just below a church and one day I went upstairs and sat before the cross and cried and cried; it's incredible to be somewhere where I'm given the space to work through my healing at my own pace. XLP does lots of work in the area where Nathaniel was killed, and although that's hard and brings back many painful memories, I know that God wants me there. It means I see Nathaniel's friends regularly, which gives me some positive reminders as well as the painful ones, and I know Nathaniel was very proud of the work that I do.

Though it's been hard to face my grief, I've realized that avoidance doesn't help at all. However painful it is, you have to face it head on and keep moving forward in the grieving process. I met another mum who lost her son in a similar way and she has stayed stuck in a time warp. She can't work; often she can't even get out of bed in the morning. She won't talk about her son at all, to anyone, and while I understand how painful it is to talk about it, it's far unhealthier to leave it all bottled up. You have to deal with the grief otherwise it takes over and destroys your entire life. There's no quick fix, of course. When you lose a child, your life is changed for ever.

I still have bad days when the sorrow overwhelms me, but when I do I try to tell myself that it's OK to feel low. You can't expect to wake up after three or four months and suddenly find life has gone back to normal. You don't just

Hannah's Story

get past the death of a child and you miss them acutely every day. The healing will be a lifelong process. I know that I can't hide my emotions from those around me, and most of all from God. I tell him how I feel and I'm honest about how much I hate what has happened. I try not to feel guilty for feeling angry but allow myself to express that anger and hope that in time it will lose its power. I still find that praying can be quite challenging and find it easier to pray for others than for myself. One thing that gives me comfort is looking up at the sky and seeing the ever-changing cloud formations. I visualize Nathaniel being up there with God and that brings me some peace. I can stay in the church service for the worship now and feel that that has been a place God has given me where I have the freedom to grieve. Sometimes it's felt like rivers of tears flowing. Many times I couldn't cope with sensing God close; it brought me to tears and it felt as if my heart would rip apart and never be put back together. But where I've felt stripped bare emotionally, it has enabled me to feel more connected to God; it's almost been like heaven touching earth. I have had amazing times of feeling God wrap me in his arms and surround me with his love – even when I didn't have the words or the energy to pray for that.

There were periods when I thought I was going to lose my mind. I felt as if I would explode with all the unanswered questions, but having people to share that with helped. I remember one day crying so much that I didn't think I would ever be able to pull myself together again, but I called a friend and she came straight over. That helped enormously; you need people who will let you feel what you're feeling and not try to tell you things are OK. I really value my friends who allow me to have both good and bad days, and who left me alone when I needed some time to grieve in private. At times it has seemed as if there would be no end to this overwhelming grief, but life does go on. I have always been known as someone who laughs a lot but for a time I thought I wouldn't ever laugh again; it was as if that part of me died with Nathaniel. But then one day, out of the blue, you find something funny again. Laughter is great therapy and sometimes I've walked the thin line between laughter and tears, but both have been gifts that have helped to heal me.

My passion for working with young people has intensified since we lost Nathaniel. At first I didn't think I could go back to my job, and without my faith, I wouldn't have been able to. I've learned the importance of sharing my story with others; we all have pain and we can all help each other. I now see with a new urgency that we must be working with young people, giving them hope and a future, and helping them to make better choices. I know more clearly than I ever imagined I would the pain that is caused by the violence in our society, but I refuse to believe this is a lost generation and I will do whatever I can to try to stop other families from suffering in the way that we have.

Chapter 9

Anger

Another side effect of suffering can be a growing feeling of anger. It's a hard emotion to deal with, as most of the things we associate with it are negative and it's rarely talked about either inside or outside the church. To me it felt a bit like worry; I thought the good "Christian" thing to do was push it aside as soon as it reared its head. Yet I was angry that I couldn't play competitive football any more; I was angry that my family have had to face a disproportionately high number of health problems in the last few years. I was angry that my life was being dominated by pain and completely disrupted by medical procedures. As I didn't know how to express that anger in a healthy way, I tried to absorb it. I did my best to squash it down but, as you'll know if you've ever tried it, that rarely ends well. I spent many days after the operation sitting on the sofa looking at the red wall of my living room (perhaps not the most helpful colour), feeling so furious that I didn't know what to do with myself. I would imagine picking objects up and hurling them at the wall and then immediately feel guilty for thinking such things. When I first tried to shower without help after the operation, I completely lost it. I was struggling to balance on my crutches and put too much weight on my broken leg (which was excruciating), and to top it off I managed to trap my fingers in the shower door. My anger built and built until I exploded and headbutted the shower door. Clearly, trying to ignore it wasn't going to work.

We know from the fact that God talks about being angry a number of times in the Bible that anger itself isn't a sin. It doesn't have to be a negative emotion. When you think about some of the things that make you angry, I wonder how many of them relate to a form of injustice. Anger can be a positive emotion showing us that something is wrong; it highlights our fundamental longing for justice, fairness, rightness, and equality. This is something that is grasped even by small children; they have a keen sense from a young age of what is and isn't fair. Anger at injustice isn't wrong, but the expression of it certainly can be. Unchecked, it can be dangerous for us and for those around us.

I'd experienced anger before, of course. I'd met orphaned children in a dirty Romanian hospital who were skeletally thin and dying from AIDS. I've spent time with parents in the UK whose children were in the wrong place at the wrong time and lost their lives. I've listened to young people tell horrific stories of the abuse they have suffered. All these situations made me angry, and that's an appropriate response. But when it came to my personal pain, I observed my problems through the filter of how they compared with situations like these, which are some of the most extreme cases of pain and injustice in the world. My problems looked like small fry in comparison, but being aware of that didn't make me feel any less angry or dull any of the pain. I had to acknowledge that, rightly or wrongly, I was angry, and I couldn't keep ignoring that fact.

Anger

All evidence suggests that suppressed anger can lead to depression, anxiety, violence, and self-harm. Anger is a normal part of the grieving process and life brings many griefs, whether it's the death of someone we love, the loss of a community we've been part of, the end of a dream we'd cherished, or the resentment at life not turning out the way we hoped it would. We're seeing more and more young people dealing with issues of anger stemming from the frustrations and difficulties in their lives. Many are dealing with intense poverty, feel they have no hope of getting a job, and have witnessed their parents' relationships fall apart. Some have been abused, or seen more violence at home than we could ever stand to watch in a film; many witness their friends being killed in drug, knife, and gun crime. There are few healthy outlets for the anger aroused by these injustices and so the young people burn with rage, some turning it in on themselves and self-harming as a twisted means of escape, others taking it out on anyone who gives them a look they don't like, perpetuating the injustice in the world. Richard Rohr, a Franciscan priest, talks about how hard it is for men in particular to express their grief, and comments, "In our work with men, we have found that in many men this inability or refusal to feel their deep sadness takes the form of aimless anger. The only way to get to the bottom of their anger is to face the ocean of sadness underneath it. Men are not free to cry, so they transmute their tears into anger, and sometimes it pools up in their soul in the form of real depression."[28]

We have to find a safe place for the anger to be released without damaging anyone. The apostle Paul says, "In your

---

[28] Richard Rohr, *Falling Upward*, London: SPCK, 2012, page 135.

anger do not sin. Do not let the sun go down while you are still angry, and do not give the devil a foothold" (Ephesians 4:26–27). In other words, he's saying the anger isn't a sin but hanging on to it is. Solomon said, "Anger resides in the lap of fools" (Ecclesiastes 7:9), with the word "resides" indicating that he means letting it become a resident rather than a visitor. For Christians there can be an additional complication of anger: what do you do when you feel angry with God? Sometimes we find ourselves in situations where we can't seem to help saying, "God, why did you let this happen?" Maybe we can see that our pain is a result of someone else's choices and we can direct our anger at them, but sometimes we still feel angry with God for the things that hurt us. We wrestle with whether he caused them to happen, whether he's in control, and whether it's ever OK to be angry with him. Thankfully, God himself gave us some direction within the Bible to allow us to understand what to do with our anger, and the Psalms are a great place to start. There we see that David (a man after God's heart – 1 Samuel 13:14) had no problems letting rip before God in his anger. He didn't hold back, with 40 per cent of the Psalms he wrote being songs of lament that expressed sorrow, confusion, and questions. People have suggested to me in the past that I try writing my own psalms of lament. When I look back on them now I realize I didn't give myself permission to be fully honest. I tried to tone down my emotions, fearing I would offend God by saying what I really thought. Before we can truly express our anger, we need to know whether it's really OK to be angry with God.

Job

When I told friends about the catalogue of problems that had occurred in my life over a few years, people started to joke that my middle name was Job. Thankfully, my life was nowhere near as bad as that of Job, who lost three daughters, seven sons, a number of servants, and a huge amount of livestock, and was then struck down with sores all over his body. Surveying the wreckage of their lives, Job's wife concluded that the only thing he could do was "Curse God and die"; to her, there seemed to be nothing else for it. Job didn't want to turn his back on God but he also couldn't pretend that everything was OK. When his friends opined that he must have done something wrong to displease God, Job maintained that he hadn't, and he dared to ask if God enjoyed oppressing him while blessing the wicked (Job 10:3). He said God had worn him out by devastating his household (16:7) and he accused God of throwing him into the mud and reducing him to dust and ash without even telling him why (30:19–20). He said that God had denied him justice (27:1) and had wronged him without explanation (19:6–7). That's some hefty criticism coming from a godly man! But when God responds, he doesn't condemn Job for his words. Instead, he tells Job's friends that they have got it wrong whereas Job spoke correctly (42:7). The incredible thing about Job was that throughout all his suffering he stayed engaged with God. When we feel hurt and angry we can either bring this before God and stay connected to him, or turn away from him and begin to let our relationship drift or be severed completely. Job raged, protested, moaned, and groaned, swinging between faith and despair, but he never gave up. He chose to trust that there was an answer even if he didn't know it. After he met God, Job repented (42:5–6). His encounter with God brought him back to his knees, where he could let go of his anger, bitterness, and pain. Getting angry with God and letting loose with the thoughts that are tearing you apart is OK. Allowing pain and bitterness to take root in your heart is a road to further pain and destruction. Engaging with God is where we find this release; pretending we're not angry means we don't engage with him or with the issues of pain and it can drive a huge wedge into our relationship with God. Anger can force us into God's presence looking for answers, and that is far healthier than allowing a detached bitterness to creep in that leads us further from him.

Pastor and author Dr Ed Stetzer tells of the agony of seeing his sister, Betty, die at the age of twenty-one. Betty was diagnosed with cancer as a young girl, and as a new believer, Ed prayed diligently that God would heal her. Betty got better for nine years before the cancer came back and took her life. Unable to comprehend why God would allow her daughter to die so young, Ed's mum walked away from the church, her Christian friends, and her relationship with God. Ed, on the other hand, demanded answers from God. He drove to the beach where he could yell and use language you wouldn't normally associate with prayer. He says, "The answers my soul craved never came. God rejected my wisdom in favour of his own. He did not give me the answers I wanted, but he gave me something better. He gave me himself instead."[29]

---

[29] Ed Stetzer, quoted in R. T. Kendall, *Totally Forgiving God*, London: Hodder & Stoughton, 2012, page xiii.

Forgiveness

Most of us would acknowledge that when someone has hurt us, we have to forgive them to be able to find freedom and healing. But how do we deal with it when we feel hurt by God? We know he has done nothing wrong yet we can be tormented by the fact that he didn't intervene and stop terrible things from happening to us. Dr R. T. Kendall was the minister at Westminster Chapel in London for twenty-five years and has written lots of bestselling books, notably *Totally Forgiving Others* and *Totally Forgiving Yourself*. A couple of years after the latter was published, a friend suggested that he should write a follow-up book called *Totally Forgiving God*. R. T. gulped, knowing that it would be easily open to misinterpretation while also knowing his friend was right. He wrote the book, and explains in it that God doesn't need to be forgiven as he wants only the best for his people and hasn't done anything wrong. Yet we live in a broken world where suffering is a reality for so many people, which can leave us feeling betrayed by God. He says, "Total forgiveness means letting everyone off the hook who has hurt us in any way. This includes God if we feel he has hurt us by allowing what he did."[30]

In my most honest moments I knew that I felt betrayed by God and that it was something I had to deal with if I was going to be able to continue in relationship with him. It didn't help that people would say, "God won't give you more than you can bear." This is a frequently quoted phrase and one that can cause great heartache to those who are suffering. When you've reached the point at which you don't feel that

---

[30] R. T. Kendall, *Totally Forgiving God*, page 158.

you can take any more and someone tells you God wouldn't give this burden to you if you couldn't handle it, it doesn't make you feel loved. Quite the opposite: it leads to further anger as you can conclude that God clearly doesn't know you all that well as you already feel beyond your breaking point. It implies that he's doling out the pain but will stop when things get too much. The phrase is actually a misquotation of Scripture; what the Bible says is that God won't allow you *to be tempted* beyond what you can bear (1 Corinthians 10:13). Paul was trying to show the Corinthians that God was with them when they were tempted and would help them find a way to resist. We need to let go of this strange image of God measuring out how much pain we can deal with, which only confuses our understanding of who he is and how he relates to us in our suffering.

Forgiving others

For some of us, it's not just God that we need to forgive. My mum is an incredible example to me of how forgiving someone else can be essential to your own freedom and emotional well-being. She was one of three children and had a very difficult upbringing. My granddad was a very violent man who couldn't hold down a job and would spend what little money they had on drink. When he came home, one wrong word or even a wrong look and he would throw things against the wall or even at my nan. My mum was twelve when he beat my nan so badly that she ended up in hospital, too frightened to tell the police what had happened. He was in and out of prison, mainly for stealing, and my mum was forced to visit him. Nan would say, "Go and kiss your dad," which meant she had to sneak cigarettes into his hands while the guards weren't looking. He had lots of affairs but my nan stayed with him for the sake of her three children and because in those days there was a real stigma attached to divorce. But eventually she couldn't take it any more and had a restraining order put on him. It was a relief that he was no longer around, but it forced them into worse poverty. They had no soap to wash with and all they could afford to eat each night were chips. They bought clothes at jumble sales and my mum had only one pair of knickers, which were washed once a week. With my nan working to try to make ends meet, my mum would often look after my uncle, who was in and out of hospital.

Over the years there was no contact between my mum and her dad and she tried to blank out as much of her past as she could because it was so painful. A few years after she became a Christian she was praying one morning and felt that God was talking to her about his being her Father. She read Psalm 139, which is such an intimate picture of a loving father, and she had a deep realization that she really belonged to God and that she was his. Having such an awful relationship with her own dad had meant that relating to God as a father was a challenge. She knew that she had to forgive her father and so she began the process of letting go of all the pain from her childhood and releasing forgiveness to him. By this time she hadn't seen him for twenty-seven years and didn't know if he was dead or alive, but she knew that if he was still living, she wanted to tell him to his face that she had truly forgiven him.

When I was sixteen, my dad was praying and asking God about some situations we were facing. He felt led to pray that my granddad would get in touch, and within a week he phoned, saying he had had a stroke and would like to see the family. We all visited together with my nan, my two uncles, and their wives, and the atmosphere was tense to say the least. All I knew was that this man had hurt my mum, so I wasn't exactly thrilled about meeting him. He had had more children and so it was very strange trying to work out who everyone was and how they related to one another. At the end of the day my dad asked if we could pray together, so we held hands and my dad prayed. I kept one eye on Mum, wanting to do all I could to stop this being painful for her. When we had finished praying, my mum walked across the room, looked her dad square in the eyes, and said, "Dad, no matter what you have done, I forgive you." I was wearing a medal I had won in a football tournament in Germany, where I was voted player of the week, and for some reason I felt compelled to take it off and give it to him. My mum says it was the first time in her life that she saw him cry. I had no idea but for him the association was with medals of honour given out during the war, and it had a deep significance for him.

We saw him only a handful of times before we received a phone call to say he had passed away. My mum not only attended the funeral but spoke at it too. I wondered what on earth she could say about him that wasn't negative. She said, "In the Bible it says you should honour your mother and father. Today I honour my dad. He gave me life and because of him I have two children of my own." My mum had every right to be angry after her traumatic and frightening childhood years, yet she was willing to forgive and let go of her anger. The process of healing can take years, especially when the hurt is deep, and forgiveness is often a choice that we have to make repeatedly, taking our anger, hurt, and pain to God. I am amazed by the depth of courage it took for her to forgive him and I'm so thankful that she didn't allow the anger and bitterness of her childhood to take root in her heart, as she wouldn't have been able to be the loving, generous, kind, and soft mum that she has been to us. She even wrote to him before his death and asked him to forgive her. I found that very difficult to understand but she said she felt she had never properly honoured him for being her dad, and that was wrong. What an incredible example of the outrageous grace that is fundamental to the gospel of Jesus. What an amazing example of the freedom and healing that was hers because she found the grace to forgive and was able to release her anger into the arms of her loving heavenly Father.

Chapter 10

Dreaming Again

When you're in the midst of a painful time, it can be hard to look to the future. Whether it's because of one huge thing or lots of small disappointments and difficulties that build up, we can begin to lose our vision. The dreams we once held dear start to fade as we lose hope that they can ever become reality. We start to ask whether we're doing something wrong; sometimes it leads us to question what our purpose is or whether we even *have* a purpose. Exhausted and despairing, we spiral down into a pit, losing sight of the hope we had.

One of the things on my horizon just before the operation was a trip to Haiti with Compassion and Spring Harvest. The country had recently been devastated by an earthquake that had claimed many lives, and I was keen to be part of something that was trying to bring relief to those people who were having to piece their lives back together. As the date drew nearer, the excitement of being involved was replaced by the dreaded realization that my body would not handle the trip. I'm the type of person who likes to "push through" as far as I can, so I hated having to cancel. I was incredibly disappointed, but once the decision was made there was also relief that I wasn't going to have to force my body to do something it clearly wasn't capable of.

Closer to home, I could still get excited about the vision of XLP but wondered, owing to the long-term nature of my condition, whether I would be able to be part of the charity's future. I felt like the person on the edge of the photo, the one who isn't quite part of the group and is on the outside looking in. I didn't know how sensible it was to dream about the future, or whether I had the energy to do it anyway. Diane said to me a number of times, "You can't see past the operations, can you?" She was right; it had become all-consuming for me. I had been a visionary leader for as long as I could remember, but what good is a visionary leader who has no vision or dreams?

One of the enemy's tactics is to steal our dreams. Vision produces energy in people by painting a picture of the future and assuring them it can become a reality. As people who love Jesus – the God of all hope – we need to believe and affirm that things can change and that we don't have to accept the status quo. We need to reimagine a world without injustice, pain, and suffering, just as we see described in Isaiah 65 and Revelation 21. These should be the things the church is known for; one of the telltale marks of God's followers should be that we're committed to making these visions a reality.

I knew that somehow I needed to go beyond the hurt, the questions, the guilt, and the anger to find a place of hope again. It was tempting to let myself get swallowed up by all that was happening and become defined by it. It was tempting to think I was useless. How could God use me when I had a huge frame strapped around my leg? Or when I could barely concentrate and was still dealing with the traumas of recent events? How could I dream, knowing I needed to go through it all again? How could he use me when I didn't know his presence? I was encouraged by the words of Steve Arterburn and Jack Felton in their book *Toxic Faith*:

> *Many fail to receive the blessing that comes from ministering to others because of the belief that God uses only the perfect or the near perfect.... In my life as well as in scripture, I have seen nothing but the opposite to be true. God uses those who have major flaws or who have been through a great deal of pain to accomplish many things for his kingdom.... No one is too messed up for God to use.*[31]

The Bishop of London said to me, "Now you have a different story to tell and you have earned the right to tell that story. What you have learned will bring hope to many." With these words ringing in my ears, I decided I needed to do what I could, even if it didn't feel like very much to me. When Mark Duggan was killed by the police in Tottenham in the summer of 2011, riots broke out across London and I was heavily involved in the press interviews. It was while I was off work with my leg that the inquest into his death took place and concluded that he was lawfully shot, despite lots of evidence that he was unarmed at the time. It was very tense and Mark Duggan's family were very upset. I was invited by the media

---

[31] Stephen Arterburn and Jack Felton, *Toxic Faith: Understanding and Overcoming Religious Addiction*, Nashville, TN: Oliver Nelson Books, 1991, pages 72–73.

to be part of the conversation again and initially I turned them down. Then I reconsidered: maybe this was a way I could contribute something – even if I did get some funny looks when I turned up at the BBC studios wearing my frame! I was also asked to go and meet the cabinet minister for civil society and said yes (though I imagined getting through the metal detectors might prove interesting), plus I had a couple of speaking engagements that we had left in the diary just in case I could make them. One was at the Pioneer Conference, where I stood up in front of 700 people and heard a huge intake of breath as I showed them my frame. I explained that I couldn't ignore it or they would have been distracted by why my trousers were so huge, so I thought I'd get it over and done with. I thought it was best to be open about where I was at too and told them about the process, saying, "This has shaken me physically, emotionally, and spiritually and yet I have had a community around me that loves me, and friends who have been there for me. The kids I work with through XLP always have many challenges themselves. Some of them grow up in the context of violence, addiction, family breakdown, exclusion from school, and sexual abuse, yet they don't have a community around them and they have to try to work it out on their own."

Even in our vulnerability and weakness we can speak up for and reach out to others. Many of you will have heard of Rick Warren, leader of Saddleback Church in the USA, which is regularly attended by 20,000 people across multiple sites. He's also the author of *The Purpose Driven Life*, which has sold more than 30 million copies since its publication in 2002. Rick and Kay Warren's son Matthew, the youngest of their three children, battled with depression for most of his life and committed suicide in 2013. The tragedy made headlines around the world and many wondered how the faith of these well-known believers would hold up in the face of such a devastating loss. In an interview with Piers Morgan on CNN, Rick was asked if he had ever doubted God or his existence. Rick replied, "No, I never did, but I doubted his wisdom." In a *Christianity* magazine article he continued, "My kids have never doubted that they had a father and that I loved them. But they've often doubted my wisdom." After Matthew's death Rick and Kay received over 5,000 letters from around the world offering condolences. They said the ones that touched them most were those who wrote that Matthew had led them to faith, saying, "I'm going to be in heaven because your son brought me to Jesus." Rick said, "'In God's garden of grace, even broken trees bear fruit.' And we are all broken... God only uses broken people."[32]

I have a complaint

Martin Luther King said, "We must accept finite disappointment, but never lose infinite hope." He was a man well acquainted with disappointment and setbacks. He received many threatening phone calls a day (many of which were death threats), he was stabbed by a mentally ill woman in New York, he suffered from exhaustion, and he spent many nights in a prison cell; a bomb went off in his home, and his volunteers were threatened, beaten, arrested, and killed. But as political activist Jim Wallis pointed out, Martin Luther King didn't stand up and say, "I have a complaint

[32] *Christianity* magazine, Premier Christian Media Trust, July 2014.

to make" or "I would like to present you with my five-year business plan". He talked about a dream of equality of peace and justice and he rallied people around that vision, painting a picture of what society could be like, and he persevered, despite everything that would have made many believe his dream was just a fantasy.

I wonder what thoughts went through his mind every time news came in of another church that had been burned down, another act of violence committed, or another life lost. I wonder if there were moments when he felt that his dream was unrealistic, or wondered whether it would be worth the cost. Even if he did, he kept going. He said, "Change does not roll in on the wheels of inevitability, but comes through continuous struggle." We have to find that bigger-picture vision of what it is we're fighting for, that God-given dream that will help us keep going despite all the odds.

But sometimes a dream from God gets confused with our personal dreams and desires. One of the most common questions I get asked by Christian young people is, "How do I know what God's will is for my life?" We're all trying to work out where we fit in to the world and what we're meant to do. And often, when we talk about our future, a particular Bible verse gets quoted: "'For I know the plans I have for you,' declares the Lord, 'plans to prosper you and not to harm you, plans to give you hope and a future'" (Jeremiah 29:11). It's one of the most frequently quoted pieces of Scripture and it's easy to see why: it's incredibly encouraging to believe that God has plans for us and that he wants good things for us. What we often fail to do, however, is to put these words into any sort of context, which means we miss out on what God was really saying.

When Faith Gets Shaken

The prophet Jeremiah's ministry covered the forty years leading up to the invasion and destruction of Jerusalem by the Babylonian army in 587 BC. Firstly, a small group was taken, along with the king and much of the treasure from the Temple; then about ten years later King Nebuchadnezzar ordered that thousands of Hebrews be marched hundreds of miles across the desert into exile in Babylon – a place where Yahweh was not known. There was no Temple of God, no Levitical sacrifices, no Hebrew festivals and celebrations, and a radically different culture. Put simply, they were aliens in a foreign land. The book of Lamentations expresses the crushing sadness they felt; they were a people who felt abandoned, rootless, vulnerable, and orphaned. In Jeremiah 28 we read the words of the prophet Hananiah, declaring that God was saying he would restore Israel and their Temple within two years, bringing back the Temple treasures that Nebuchadnezzar had taken to Babylon. This was the prophecy the people were longing for and Jeremiah would have been happy to see it fulfilled, only it wasn't a word from God. It was against this backdrop that Jeremiah wrote a letter from Jerusalem to the elders, priests, prophets, and all the people who had been exiled. He told them they would be in exile for seventy years, so they should settle down and plan to stay. For a people desperately longing to go home, these were no easy words to hear; Hananiah's two years were far more appealing. Yet, in God's amazing way, this seventy years wasn't to be wasted time; God had a purpose within it.

> *This is what the Lord Almighty, the God of Israel, says to all those I carried into exile from Jerusalem to*

> *Babylon: "Build houses and settle down; plant gardens and eat what they produce. Marry and have sons and daughters; find wives for your sons and give your daughters in marriage, so that they too may have sons and daughters. Increase in number there; do not decrease. **Also, seek the peace and prosperity of the city to which I have carried you into exile. Pray to the Lord for it, because if it prospers, you too will prosper.**"*
>
> Jeremiah 29:4–7 (Emphasis mine)

It was in this context that God promised his people a hope and a future (Jeremiah 29:11). As David Lamb, an author and professor of the Old Testament, points out,[33] these words were offered to a group of people in incredible pain who were undergoing a huge transition from their own land to being enslaved, and yet God spoke hope into their situation. He notes that the "you" in Jeremiah 29:11 is actually plural, meaning "you all", as it was written to a community and not an individual. Despite all that they had lost, the people were still in it together, and God would bless them as a community as they sought the welfare of the whole community and as they embraced his plan. We see this truth all over Scripture that God intended us for community, right from the start of Genesis where he declares it is not good for man to be alone (Genesis 2:18) to Jesus sending the disciples out in twos, through to the incredible model of community we see in Acts. We're meant to do this life together, draw strength from one another, and support each other through the good and the bad times.

---

[33] David Lamb, *God Behaving Badly: Is the God of the Old Testament Angry, Sexist and Racist?*, Downers Grove, IL: IVP, 2011.

Inspiration

The nature of suffering is such that it often turns our thoughts inwards. When it's taking every ounce of our energy just to make it through the day, it can be hard to look outwards and attend to the needs of others. One person who really inspired me with the way he handled suffering was my Uncle Alan. He was my mum's younger brother, so he too suffered a traumatic upbringing, at my grandad's hands just like my mother. He was just six months old when he got double pneumonia and was diagnosed with severe asthma, meaning he was in and out of hospital and had to have lots of time off school over the years, so his education suffered. In his twenties he had oxygen therapy and was given steroids to help with the pain; he had a lower lobe of one lung removed and had a major haemorrhage, so had to be taken back into hospital. Five years later he woke up one day with a frozen shoulder, which was diagnosed as chronic arthritis, and it spread everywhere, causing him severe pain. He had to have surgery to realign his fingers and toes, and needed knee replacements. Later he was diagnosed with chronic obstructive pulmonary disease, which is common in smokers – only Uncle Alan didn't smoke. He was often breathless, had a persistent cough with phlegm, and had frequent chest infections; doctors predicted he wouldn't live past fifty. Alan had every right to feel bitter and angry and to let his illness define his life. Yet despite these challenges he was great to be around, and when I was young he used to take me to watch Tottenham play. He got married and had two girls, and his faith was very important to him. He became a foster carer for high-risk children, sometimes looking after them for a few days, sometimes for a few years. He became a DJ on hospital radio with his own show, called Magic Hobbs; he wanted to give something back to the place that had looked after him as a patient so many times. He did have some very low days and we knew we could never understand the full extent of the challenges he was facing. He was a very generous and kind man, who never held back from telling me he was proud of me even when he was lying in a hospital bed dying.

At his funeral over 200 people gathered to pay their respects and tell stories of how Alan had made a difference in their lives. There were kids for whom he'd performed puppet shows at Christmas, postmen that he'd worked with, and many family and friends, all testifying to a life well lived despite everything that was thrown at him. My Uncle Alan wasn't like Martin Luther King; he didn't have a huge dream that would transform society and change history, but he still managed to dream that, despite the pain he was in every day, he could make a difference to other people's lives. He wasn't defined by his illness and suffering and that's one of the reasons he will always stand in my memory as an example of what we can overcome.

You might also remember the recent example of Stephen Sutton. When Stephen was fifteen he was diagnosed with bowel cancer. Despite rigorous treatment the cancer kept growing, and a few years later he was told it was terminal. Rather than asking the doctors how long he had left to live, he decided to measure his time by how much of a difference he could make. So he made a "bucket list" of forty-six things he wanted to do before he died, including raising £10,000 for the Teenage Cancer Trust. When Stephen posted what he thought would be a final message on his Facebook page, showing a picture of him giving a thumbs-up from his hospital bed, the post went viral and suddenly the money came pouring in. So many people were touched by Stephen's story that he ended up raising over £4 million. In a typical show of character, he said, "I might be a young person with cancer but cancer doesn't have to have me. It's not the cancer that defines who I am but how I react to it." Stephen's attitude and actions touched the lives of many, inspiring us all to live life to the full. He said, "I don't have the time to help others but I have the motivation. You have the time but maybe you don't have the motivation, so maybe I can give you the motivation." That, perhaps more than the £4 million, may well be Stephen's legacy. What an inspirational and challenging example to us all.

I'm amazed by the strength of the human spirit that enables people to hang on to hope despite the bleakest of circumstances. I've been hugely privileged to visit a number of countries through my work, such as India, Ghana, Jamaica, Bolivia, and many others. Though I have travelled with the hope of blessing others, I've usually ended up being more blessed in return. One thing that has always struck me about some of the incredibly poor communities I've been to is that people really rely on one another. They don't have a sense of competition or ego, but deeply value relationships and teamwork. They have learned to wait and not demand everything in an instant, as we so easily find ourselves doing here. They know what it is to worship God in all circumstances and so the changing of their circumstances doesn't result in a crisis of faith. There is something pure and attractive about their faith that I long to discover again for myself. I have seen it here in the UK too when I've worked with families who have lost children to gun and knife crime and yet seen their suffering cause them to go deeper in their faith. Many tell me that without their faith they would have no hope. Though they are still hurting and often angry and confused, they hang on to their faith as though it is a life raft, and they don't let go. Many of them have set up foundations and charities that seek to provide opportunities for young people in inner-city communities. They haven't let their hopes and their dreams die with their children; instead, they've been inspired by their own tragedy to reach out and help others. I can't help but be astonished by such a gracious response to suffering. I am constantly amazed by people's ability to trust in such adversity and to keep their dreams alive in the midst of such pressures.

I read a story of a young man and his wife who had been trying to have a child for five years without any joy. They were consumed by the pain and exhaustion of their journey, wondering why God hadn't given them a child and why he remained silent. Finally there was a miracle – the wife became pregnant! A few months later and the joy doubled: they were having twins! They rejoiced in God's goodness and felt hugely blessed; even the years of waiting didn't seem to matter. But then tragedy struck. During a routine check-up it was discovered that one of the babies had died and the other was unlikely to survive; they were advised to abort. How could God do this? What kind of God gives you a gift and then snatches it away from you? Grieving and devastated, they felt their faith was hanging by a thread. The husband was encouraged by friends at church to go on a silent retreat, where one of the spiritual exercises was a nature walk to look for God in the everyday. Angry and hurting, the man thought it was a waste of an hour and decided he would walk only on a long concrete path where he wouldn't have to see anything natural. He said:

> *I was about halfway along the path, walking very slowly, lost in anger and resentment of God, when tears began… There were cracks in the concrete… in every crack, a flower somehow in the midst of the grey lifeless concrete, life made its way through impenetrable rock and mortar of the pavement! Suddenly I was conscious of God. He was alive! He surprised me with flowers. He found a way to show me hope in the midst of despair, His love and care found me.*[34]

Even while this man was so lost in his own despair and grief, even while he was rejecting God, God gave him a picture of love and hope. No matter what happens, no matter how badly we're hurting, and how badly we want to get angry at God or how tempted we are to fall into a hopeless existence, we are loved by God. There is always hope because he is always with us. Sometimes when we're struggling to hang on to this for ourselves, we can find truth in the words and prayers of others. While I was finding it hard knowing how to ask God to reignite my hope and help me dream for the future, I pinned this prayer by St Brendan onto my wall:

---

[34] Mike Yaconelli, *Messy Spirituality*, London: Hodder & Stoughton, 2001, page 154.

Dreaming Again

I determine amidst all uncertainty always to trust.
I choose to live beyond regret, and let you recreate my life.
I believe you will make a way for me
   And provide for me,
If only I trust
And obey.
I will trust in the darkness and know that my times are
   still in your hand.
I will believe you for my future,
Chapter by chapter, until all the story is written…
Teach me to live with eternity in view,
Tune my spirit to the music of heaven.

Chapter 11

VSP

Last year we received a call in the office to say that Desmond Tutu, the world-renowned, Nobel-prize-winning social rights activist, and Mary Robinson, the former president of Ireland, wanted to come to visit XLP. It was a huge honour, but most of the young people we work with had no idea who they were or why they wanted to come and see them. With their arrival scheduled for 10 a.m. on a Tuesday, we were seriously worried that all our young people would be either in school or still in bed. So the team knocked on their doors and tried to persuade them that it would be good for them to meet an 81-year-old man from South Africa whom they'd never heard of. We took the bus that we use for outreach to one of the local estates we visit each week, and thankfully it was packed full when Tutu arrived. When he got out of the taxi, he grabbed hold of my hand and didn't let go (much to the amusement of the young people!). I thought he would sock it to them about the real nature of poverty and being oppressed, but instead Tutu made it clear he was there to listen. The young people began to open up, telling him how having a certain postcode ruined their chances of getting a job, how hard it was to see your dad beat your mum up and not be able to stop him, what it's like looking after your younger siblings when you're just a teenager yourself, how it feels to see your

VSP

best friend get stabbed and killed. Tutu listened intently to each person's story and then he said, "What you need to realize, more than anything else, is that your past doesn't have to define your future." He grabbed the hand of one of the boys whose mate had been killed a year before and said, "I'll tell you what you are: a VSP – a very special person. You're made in the image of God and you have the potential to change the world." The guy was speechless as he was told his true worth. Even as I stood there I felt as if God was saying to me, "That's how I feel about you," and it completely blew me away. It's easy to see how someone else is special but sometimes harder to accept that God thinks we are too.

Later on, Tutu gave a speech at a different event we were both speaking at, and he said, "There were moments visiting XLP where you felt your heartstrings were being tugged, you were very close to tears, looking at these young people who could have been going down a cul-de-sac but then they realized what incredible potential they have when given the chance to blossom. Each one of these kids is a masterpiece; God doesn't create rubbish, each one of us is special to God, and your name is engraved on his hands. The most important thing you can do is to remind people they are special to God."

Before he left at the end of the day, Tutu turned to me and said, "You make God smile." Wow. That simple phrase wouldn't leave me afterwards. For all the ways I was beating myself up, God was telling me I was a VSP in his eyes and that I made him smile. It's amazing how many of us find it easier to believe the negative things about ourselves. Sometimes they are lies other people have spoken about us, ways that people have made us feel that we've let them down, or areas where we're just too self-critical. I'm learning that I can't control what other people think of me. Even when I do my best, people may still judge me and find me wanting; I can't make everyone happy, but I need to listen to what God is saying about me, not other people and not my inner critic. Letting go of these judgments involves trusting God at a deeper level and choosing to tune in to his voice, allowing his to be the loudest in my life.

It's not about us

Being a keen footballer from a young age, I grew up acutely aware that I was judged on my performance. I liked playing centre forward as there were plenty of opportunities to score, but of course if you didn't score for a couple of games in a row, the pressure was really on. It seemed that it didn't matter how well you played; it only mattered if you scored. Performing well became how I got my sense of worth.

I'm sure you've heard as many times as I have that God loves you for who you are, not for what you do. I've heard the sermons, and even *given* the sermons, and yet I'm not sure I actually live in the reality of that truth. It's a long process for many of us to let go of the ways we're judged by the world and learn to feel loved and valued just as we are. It can be even harder to believe that you are loved when you're going through periods of suffering and pain or seeing your loved ones going through them. It's easy to feel that you're not as valuable when you're not able to give as much, or to believe that God is blessing those he loves and you've somehow fallen short.

Sometimes I wonder if I need to cut God some slack. I know that if my kids doubted I love them I would be absolutely heartbroken. It would hurt so much to think they believed I loved them because of how well they did in school tests or in an athletics race. For the first few years of their lives they mainly kept me awake night after night, puked on my clothes, made me watch endless episodes of *Balamory* until the theme tune was permanently etched on my memory, and caused me embarrassment by having tantrums in public. They drove me to the edge of sanity and if any of my friends had done even one of these things, I don't think we'd have stayed friends for long. Yet, with my kids, none of those things altered my love for them at all. I am their dad. I hope that they know by my words and through my actions that they are loved, simply because I am their father. Even when they are angry and frustrated with me, I hope they still trust in the fact that my love for them never changes.

When we suffer, we often start to question why God would allow this suffering to come into our lives if he truly loved us. I remember hearing Rob Parsons at Spring Harvest[35] talking about how, when we were young, many of us used to pull petals from a daisy to help us decide whether the boy or girl we liked loved us back. With each petal removed we'd say, "S/he loves me, s/he loves me not", until the last petal determined which it was. Rob suggested that we often treat God the same way: "I got a promotion at work – God loves me; I had a car accident – he loves me not. I got to go out with the girl I have had my eye on for ages – he loves me; I didn't

---

[35] Heard at Spring Harvest, but also to be found in Wayne Jacobsen, *He Loves Me!: Learning to Live in the Father's Affection*, Nashville, TN: FaithWords, 2008.

get the job I wanted – he loves me not. I got the opportunity I've been longing for to lead at church – he loves me; I am really sick – he loves me not." Our belief in God's love for us sways with the wind of circumstance. Instead, we have to fix our eyes on Jesus (as we're reminded to in Hebrews 12:2) and remember the cross. It is there, in the face of the saviour who died for us, that we see all we need to know about God's love.

When we look at our circumstances we can get confused about God's character, but when we look at the life of Jesus we see a God who doesn't stand back and watch his people suffering. He enters into their lives, he seeks them out, he offers grace and unconditional love; he gives absolutely everything that he has to give in order that we might know we're loved. When we doubt that God is with us, we have to cling on to the truth that he has promised never to leave us (Hebrews 13:5). When we fear that the pain will break us and there's no hope, we have to hold on to the fact that God is still working for our good despite the things going on around us (Romans 8:28). When we wonder whether God really loves us, we can read Romans 8:31–39 and remember that there are no circumstances that can stop him from loving us. This is why reading our Bibles and praying is so important – not to check something off on our spiritual to-do list but to get to know God. The more we know him, the more time we spend with him, the more we invite him into our lives, the greater the trust we have in who he is, no matter what.

Imagine what life might be like if we really knew who God was, and the truth that he loves us and that we belong to him. Imagine being free from the need to impress anyone. Imagine not having to achieve anything to feel valued. Imagine your self-esteem not being changed according to how funny, intelligent, successful, or attractive others deem you to be. Imagine being able to love even those who disapprove of you. Imagine being able to love others fully because you know you are fully loved.

Looking to the future

It feels as if my life is on a bit of a loop and I'm now back where I was at the start of this book, trying to decide when to have my second leg broken and go through the whole process again. Am I in enough pain to warrant the operation? Should I try to hang on a bit longer? What will happen to XLP while I'm out of action? What toll will all this take on my family? Will I react better this time or will it take me to breaking point again? Will the frame have to be on longer than last time (as the consultant likes to remind me: each operation is different), and will I manage to avoid pin-site infections again? How much more complicated will the MRSA make things? People keep asking if it's easier or harder knowing what is going to happen, and the truth is a little of both. I still have lots of unanswered questions but I'm slowly learning to accept the uncertainty and trust that God is for me and with me, whether I feel him or not. I'm trying to keep my eyes on Jesus rather than on the things going on around me so that I stay anchored to him and secure in my faith.

In many ways I was nervous about writing this book. I didn't want to pretend to be an expert on any of these areas I've talked about, as I'm just an ordinary guy who is still very much going through the process of working things out. In some ways it has been the most difficult book I have written and it has certainly made me feel the most vulnerable. I'm passionate about loving God, loving others, and learning to love myself, so I just wanted to be honest about some of my struggles. I wanted to show you some of the "behind-the-scenes" parts of my life because I know there are many of you who are facing similar difficulties and I think it helps if we're honest about them. Church and Christian community shouldn't be somewhere we have to plaster on an "Everything is great" smile; it should be the place we can be real. What ultimately motivated me to put pen to paper was meeting others on a similar journey to me, and I genuinely hope that you have found some help through the pages of this book.

I pray that, whatever you are going through, you will know you are not on your own; God is with you. I pray you will be able to trust him and know that in your brokenness you are held together by his love. I pray that you will continue to show courage and vulnerability, allowing others close enough to you to share in your journey. I pray that you will find God's peace that allows you to feel like the bird in the midst of the storm: safe despite all that is going on around you. I pray you will be kind to yourself and exercise some self-compassion, giving yourself a break when you need it and not beating yourself up with "should, ought, must, never, and always". I pray you won't internalize your anger but will, where necessary, be able to forgive others, yourself, and God for the suffering you've experienced. I pray that hope will rise in you and you will be able to dream again, aligning your dreams with God's big dream. Most of all, I pray that you will know deep in your heart that God has created you as a Very Special Person and that you will learn to live in this Father's love that knows no bounds.

VSP

This poem is based on text found scrawled on a cellar wall in Cologne, Germany, in 1943. It is believed to have been written by a child hiding from the Nazis:

I believe in the sun,
even when it is not shining.
And I believe in love,
even when there's no one there.
And I believe in God,
even when He is silent.
I believe through any trial,
there is always a way.
But sometimes in this suffering
and hopeless despair,
My heart cries for shelter,
to know someone's there.
But a voice rises within me, saying, 'Hold on
my child, I'll give you strength,
I'll give you hope. Just stay a little while.'[36]

---

[36] Author unknown, public domain.

Epilogue

Beauty from Brokenness

As I said, I was nervous about sharing this story. I feared some might judge me and my faith (or lack of it). I worried they might think I was weak. As soon as I sent the manuscript off to be published I doubted the wisdom of putting some of my most private thoughts and fears into a book for anyone to see. Waves of shame would hit me out of nowhere, rolling over me and telling me I should have kept quiet. To say I felt vulnerable doesn't come close.

It didn't take long to see people's reaction. Within weeks the messages came rolling in, and people weren't condemning me but saying "me too": I've felt like this; I've experienced this type of pain and confusion; and I've been longing for someone to talk about it in church.

I had worried people really wanted an expert to help them in their pain and suffering; it turns out they just wanted someone who was willing to hold their hand up and say they were hurting too. I started to hear story after story of incredible people going through heartbreaking suffering. I was floored by their ability to keep going, to keep getting up every day and put one foot in front of the other. I was amazed by their bravery and their willingness to help others despite their own struggles.

What spoke to me the most was that people were willing to be honest and vulnerable just because I had been honest and vulnerable. There was a power in breaking the silence.

We took this book on tour and the same thing happened. People let their guard down and shared their stories. We laughed and we cried together and we brought our most painful moments to the foot of the cross, trying to hold on to the fact that we are loved just as we are. Time and time again I heard the same thing, "Not enough people are talking about this." It made me realize this part of my story wasn't over: God was calling me to keep being honest, to keep sharing my pain and to reach out to others in theirs.

A new dream

Diane and I started to dream. We dreamed about a world where mental and emotional health would be understood and accepted in safe and supportive communities and in which everyone could grow and flourish. We thought about the fact that the church is in every community in this country and will outlast politicians and governments in its ability to work relationally with people. We got really passionate about the Japanese art of *kintsugi* where cracked pots are mended using a golden glue. It makes a feature of the broken places instead of trying to hide them, and the result is beautiful. As we began to talk about *kintsugi* with people, particularly with friends who weren't in church, we realized it connected with others too. But what could we do?

We were tired; our journey had taken its toll on us. I'd already started one charity from scratch so I knew all about the stress it involved. Back then when I began XLP it was just me to clothe and feed; now Diane and I have four kids, two dogs, a cat, and a mortgage. The second operation on my knee had to happen and it took me out of action for nine months battering us again with the physical, mental, and emotional trauma it involved. My anxiety showed no signs of abating. Many would wisely say it wasn't the ideal time to start something new. Yet God seemed to be speaking to us and stirring our hearts.

So we started studying movements that had begun at a grassroots level and had managed to create a sense of belonging. We looked at things like parkrun, Rock Choir, Weight Watchers, Slimming World, and Alcoholics Anonymous. We would stay up late at night talking about how amazing it would be to create spaces where people could be real and honest; places that made them feel safe and supported. Diane began to write a twelve-week programme on well-being and we thought we'd try it out as a life group. We invited a few friends to join us and were amazed that they said yes. When we chatted to other parents on the playground they started opening up:

> *"Yeah, I'm broken; my husband has just left."*
> *"I'm in debt and no one knows."*
> *"I'm an alcoholic."*
> *"I suffer from anxiety."*

We were stunned. These were people we had seen almost every day for years and we had no idea what was going on in their lives. Our life group trebled in size. The first week we crowded in to our front room, everyone chatting nervously, not quite knowing what to expect. I was as nervous as anyone.

Diane said to everyone, "Turn to the person next to you and ask them about a high point and a low point in their life."

I was sat beside a guy I'd known my whole life in church and we started to talk. Words began pouring out of his mouth, telling me about things that had happened to him that I had no idea about. I learned more about him in those five minutes than I had from decades of being in the same church as him. All I could say when he finished was, "I'm sorry." I was sorry for the pain he'd been through – but more than that I was sorry that we'd created and sustained a culture where we don't truly know people or the reality of what they're dealing with. We offered each other comfort in what we were facing, and it was clear that the same thing was happening across the room: people were opening up and letting others in.

The beautiful thing was that there was no "them" and "us". Diane and I weren't there to fix anyone or give them answers; we felt just as broken as them. It brought home in a new way the truth that we need to let go of the labels of "those in need" and "those who are able to help". We're *all* in need and we can *all* help. The group gave us a forum to love and support one another. No one needed to be rescued by us – only Jesus can rescue people. No one needed to be changed – again, Jesus is the one who does that. We just wanted to create a community where unity and diversity were both possible. We wanted to love people.

Something amazing happened over those weeks we met together. Not only did people keep coming back but we all began to grow and thrive. For me, doing the programme underlined that we are more alike than we sometimes realize. One significant exercise for me was when we all wrote down our biggest fear on a piece of paper without letting anyone else see. We put the paper in an envelope and put it in the middle of the table, then all of our envelopes were mixed up. We then took it in turns to read out someone else's fear and discussed what advice we would give the person struggling with that fear. My biggest fear is health anxiety and it's often felt like a lonely thing, so imagine how I felt when four out of the ten of us who were there that night also wrote "health anxiety"! I realized I'm not alone and we even laughed together about how many times we've used Google to try to diagnose our latest symptom!

I learned so much from the group and felt truly humbled to be part of it. As the programme started to come to a close we began to make plans for curry nights and doing pub quizzes together; no one wanted the camaraderie to end. What was lovely too was that some of those who were not part of our original life group decided to stay even when the content changed back to a more traditional Bible study. The relationships they had formed had been special and they wanted to continue to support their new friends as well as to be supported by them. It felt to me like the common saying that people should feel like they belong before they believe was coming to life.

The seed had been planted for me and Diane: wouldn't it be amazing to pilot the programme in other places and see if it was helpful elsewhere? We started to talk to other churches who were interested in running it in their community and began to provide them with training. We kept in touch to support them and they were buzzing about what was happening in their groups. Before long the well-being programme was running in people's homes, in cafes, in churches, in homeless hostels, prisons, and schools – and in each place people were starting to let down their defences, acknowledge their weaknesses and struggles, build community, and support one another.

When I think about what makes these groups work I like to draw on the teaching of a well-known philosopher – Winnie-the-Pooh – who is quoted as wisely saying:

> *Don't walk behind me, I may not lead.*
> *Don't walk in front of me, I may not follow.*
> *Just walk beside me and be my friend.*

A new charity

Diane and I found our longing to do more in the area of mental health growing and we were passionate about expanding the work we were doing. I handed over XLP and we began a charity called Kintsugi Hope in order to focus our efforts on helping people's mental well-being.

My prayer at the time was,

> *God, I can't deal with another move of your Spirit that happens in a warehouse in America with a famous evangelist claiming there is revival. I want to see a move of your Spirit in prisons and coffee shops, schools and hospitals, pubs and parks, where ordinary people just come and meet you. Could there be a revival that isn't led by those with the biggest marketing budget to gather a crowd, but one that's led by the humble, the broken, the courageous, and the vulnerable?*

As well as training churches to run Kintsugi Hope well-being groups, we started to do tours and speak at various events and conferences. We have remained committed to working and supporting people internationally whose mental and emotional health has been affected by conflict, trauma, and poverty, particularly within the refugee community. This has recently seen us undertake trips to Iraq, visiting trauma centres and speaking to refugees, and to Trench Town in Jamaica, continuing the relationship with a school there where the children suffer from serious neglect and gun violence is rife. We also do advocacy work, speaking to the press, politicians, policy-makers, and think tanks to represent the lives of those we work with and to continue to raise the issues around mental health.

There is a small team of us at Kintsugi Hope now. My amazing PA messaged me one day and said, "I'm going to teach you a new word: flawsome. It means an individual who embraces their flaws and knows they're awesome, regardless." I loved that and have used it ever since. We are all flawsome. We are all broken and if we are going to receive help we need to let go of our pride and be able to admit it. But we are all beautiful too because beauty comes out of brokenness, just like the stunning *kintsugi* works of art. A key tagline we use around Kintsugi Hope is "Discovering treasure in life's scars" because that's what we want to help people see. Life may sometimes be full of pain and heartbreak and suffering but there is also beauty and love and joy.

Find out more at **www.kintsugihope.com**

See the strength in your scars and how hardship can become fuel for a more hopeful future

Bouncing Forwards

Notes on resilience, courage and change

Patrick Regan
with Liza Hoeksma

Available Now
9780281089338 • Paperback • 156 Pages

spck group

We've all had times when we're desperate to know that brighter days are ahead

'Timely, insightful and practical'
Dr Chi-Chi Obuaya, Consultant Psychiatrist

Brighter Days

12 steps to strengthening your wellbeing

Patrick Regan
with Liza Hoeksma

Available Now
9780281087877 • Paperback • 192 Pages

spck group